The Senate of Lilliput

EDWARD PEARCE

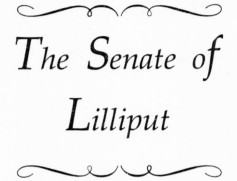

The Senate of Lilliput

ff

FABER & FABER
London   Boston

First published in 1983
by Faber & Faber Limited
3 Queen Square London WC1N 3AU
Printed in Great Britain by
Redwood Burn Ltd Trowbridge
All rights reserved

British Library Cataloguing in Publication Data

Pearce, Edward
The Senate of Lilliput.
1. Great Britain. Parliament. House of Commons—
Anecdotes, facetiae, satire, etc.
I. Title
328.41'072'0207   JN550
ISBN 0-571-13158-1

For my Mother, Deanna and Cecily

Contents

Acknowledgements

I would like to acknowledge the enormous trouble taken in retyping my original typescript by my wife Deanna, who has also prepared the index, and by the *Daily Telegraph* parliamentary correspondents' indispensable secretary, Sally Hallam. Thanks are owing too to certain Members of Parliament, whose anonymity is guaranteed.

E.P.
January 1983

1

The Arena

After prayers they start fighting.

I refer of course to Members of Parliament. One looks into the chamber and sees them at their appointed places. Here a Minister and a coven of his deputies clutching their clip-in folders which contain the typed answers to oral questions. Behind on the second Government bench sits the Minister's Parliamentary Private Secretary occasionally ferrying the odd piece of paper which the appropriate civil servants, secluded in their own sub-gallery like women in a synagogue, may have slipped through helpful back-bench hands. Ministers do cope with the fairly modest task which is set them—some primly, some reading the brief as if it were one of the Church of England's more awful new forms of service; others with a touch of flash, seeking a little light reputation in the singed flesh of combat.

Behind are the back-benches—four of them, containing the hopeful and the sycophantic, the rule-breakers and the heavy-metal technicians of uproar, outrage and suspension. Some, but by no means all of these sit below the gangway which divides each side of the House. The front row below the gangway on both sides has tended to become a refuge for desperate men, Alsatias for those who have opted out of the gerbil race for the rank of Junior Minister and above. It contains the like of Alan Clark, Dennis Skinner, Bob Cryer, Sir John Biggs-Davison and Dennis Canavan. They are people who have little in common except a desire to beat the place up, a torrential contempt for Mr Edward Heath and Mr Roy Jenkins and any other persons with affectations of eminence who expect to be listened to in conditions of penitential hush because they are

Important People making Valuable Statements. Between the two Alsatias there is, give or take the odd affectionate cry of 'Fascist' or 'KGB', very little real ill feeling. They are not respectable, these chaps.

Unfortunately for themselves, the Social Democrats have taken it into their heads to seize the front bench below the gangway. Though 'seize' is a somewhat butch word for a party given over to so much limp-wristed velleity. It was a mistake. It was rather like a church fête being held in Pentonville.

There are, you see, twenty-four microphones strung from the ceiling serving the 635 MPs who might theoretically be in the House. And while twenty-four is quite enough there has to be some clustering. The Social Democrats by choosing the front bench below the gangway have obliged poor Mr Jenkins to share a microphone with Mr Dennis Skinner. In consequence thoughtful and stimulating disquisitions, which for a few hundred pounds a go might have filled up the pages of *The Times* without anybody noticing, are subjected to a sort of ruffianly running commentary.

The Liberals sit in the row behind—laconic Jo, gambling-house Clement, cement-sack Cyril and the boy David, as comprehensive a parliamentary flop as he is a television sensation. The difference is that the television audience is full of mothers to whom the hard-faced little idealist can come over as the son they ought to have had. The Commons by contrast is full of tall uncaring males with expert ears, for whom those cassette sermons are not reasonable and fair-minded but vaguely reminiscent of a school monitor on chapel duty. And of course it is also Mr Steel's misfortune to sit behind Mr Skinner and to suffer the death of a thousand mumbles.

MPs sit in the House in little clutches of the like-minded. There is a group of Tory right-wingers usually to be found in or about Mr Nick Budgen, the umbrella-shaped member for Wolverhampton South-West, who occupies the remotest back bench, back symbolically to the wall and straddling the gangway. In the back benches level with the Speaker and out of sight of the back gallery sits a group of Midlands Labour MPs. These, based on a nucleus of Mr Jeff Rooker and Mr Peter Snape, are the anti-Benn Left, a subdivision within the Soft Left. In the back seats at the furthest end of the House from the Speaker tends to be found the Unspeakable Left, pro-Soviet and a little confused about whether to be pro-Vietnam or pro-Cambodia, a distancing that Mr Thomas finds agreeable.

There is a place for the aspiring too. The third and fourth rows above the gangway on the Tory side are occupied by the sort of people whose respectful interventions, often accompanied by the washing of hands in invisible water, about their gratitude to the Minister for his most valuable decision, bring forth cries of 'Give him a job' and little shrugs of irritation from the subtler front-bench objects of such creative humility. Former Ministers have a taste for the third row below the gangway when they can get it. And Mr James Callaghan, who periodically intervenes to show Mr Foot how to lead the Labour Party, has also settled for that spot since the ex-Prime-Ministerial pedestal—first seat below the gangway on the front row—would involve the sort of rough trade just described. It would also bring him into a proximity with the Social Democrats far more demonstrative of the standpoint of a discreet well-wisher than would be altogether wise.

Mr Heath of course, when he can be bothered, occupies the official residence—first front-bench seat below the gangway on the Government side, i.e., to the Speaker's right. From there, give or take the odd wink to Labour when Mrs Thatcher has troubles, he maintains an expression of stupendous displeasure. Mr Heath, in the light-coloured suits which are so much at odds with his weight problem, trying with so little success to look expressionless, is a sort of decoration—a caryatid with nothing to support.

On the fourth bench below the gangway on the Opposition side (on the Speaker's left) sit half a dozen grim-faced Ulster Protestants including that honorary grim-faced Ulster Protestant, Mr Enoch Powell. Mr Powell, who during the filibuster against the 1982 Prior Bill managed to make seventeen speeches in one day, is, as the cliché puts it, a good House of Commons man. And he is present for two purposes, sedulously to do his duty by Northern Ireland, and then, by way of a non-optional extra, to make interventions in broader all-British politics. One would not say that, as an early advocate of honest money and a foreign policy with a modest pro-British element in it, he is actually pleased to find that he must play Moses to Mrs Thatcher's Aaronette, but it is a sight better than circular manoeuvres in the wilderness.

One cannot talk about the House, about the arena of political dispute, without some account of the Speakership. There was once a tradition that the office of Speaker should be seized by whichever party found itself with a working majority rather as, after staging a *coup d'état*, one would grab the radio station and play records of martial music. Towards the end of the eighteenth century this tradition was modified, not least by Mr Speaker Fletcher Norton who kept a crate of beer under the Chair. For a long time in the nineteenth century it was a job for heavy Christian lawyers with an excessive sense of the dignity of things. Today the dignity of the House is somewhat diminished, to the rage, it would seem, of the public who have responded to the shambolic uproar of broadcast proceedings with an indignation which suggests a regrettable seriousness of mind.

The Speaker and his immediate predecessors occupy a middle

position. Naturally they don't want barbarous, stupid nastiness such as comes from the atrocious Mr Ron Brown (Leith, to be distinguished from the temperate Mr Ron Brown, Hackney South and Shoreditch). Yet, like the sketch writers, they actually *need* a measure of trouble. Any conscientious policeman likes to have some collar or other to put a finger on. And what is the use of keeping order if the MPs could keep it without you? When Dennis Skinner was ill the welcome he received from Mr Thomas on his return was deeply moving; and, being fully recovered, he was thrown out again within weeks.

Not often does one observe real rage of the kind which in 1912 had an Ulster Member throwing at Mr Churchill's head a book which turned out to be a guide to correct parliamentary conduct. The disorder with which I am familiar is of a measured, ritualistic kind, though if the black-leather element of the Militant Tendency wins many seats public unpleasantness of an unsatirical kind could take place.

However it is important to remember that the Speaker has a great deal of peremptory power. You start a row, he warns you. You carry on, he asks you to leave. You carry on carrying on and he names you. That is, he says, with all the Welsh irascibility he can manage, 'I name Mr Bert Briggs' or, altogether less probably, 'Mr Montague Lascelles' (for the Tories seem either smarter or meeker); up jumps the government Chief Whip and formally moves that Mr Briggs/ Lascelles be suspended from the House. Usually it is not contested, though when Mr Andrew Faulds threw his rubber duck out of the cot during one of the Falklands sessions somebody on the St Giles Rookery bench formally opposed with a seconder and the whole thing was taken to a division.

A good Speaker is a nice balance of sherry-serving college tutor and the fear of hell. For there are occasions when authority does come close to breaking down. The reaction to the Industrial Relations Act was a case in point—the union-payroll vote and the Ozymandian soul of Edward Heath met at the point of combustion. Under pressure the Speaker is on his feet doing the 'Order, Order' bit for real. And when he *is* on his feet everybody else is supposed to be sitting down. Usually, but not quite always, that works at least for a while. *In extremis* and invariably to the private black-marking of the Speaker by the *cognoscenti*, the House is suspended. The normal time is half an hour—cooling-off time as they call it in American labour legislation—but come the Apocalypse Mr Thomas can stop play for the day. Only once, ninety years ago in the unhappy, Irish-belaboured time of Mr Speaker Gully, were the Metropolitan Police summoned.

What any sensible Speaker wants is a modest amount of riot every now and again which he can be seen quelling thus giving cause for murmurs in the whips' offices of 'Good old Fred. Has the measure of the House, y'know.'

The personality of the Speaker matters vastly. For most, trouble is scotched in the foothills of disaster, commonly by a joke. And, at the risk of taking a cosy view of politics, Mr Thomas truly has been outstanding. He is short on self-importance and a lot of his better jokes are at his own expense. At the same time he is a nice man whom people don't want to upset. It is humbug, or at least half humbug to talk about respecting the Chair in some etiolated, mystical way as if it were the Holy Ghost. If the occupant of the Chair is a dull functionary or even if, despite virtues, he lacks political fingertips, trouble is altogether more likely. If for any reason Mr Speaker has a body of enemies in the House, he can have the mind of Max Planck and the thigh muscles of Nijinsky and be a disaster.

I would offer shortening odds against the present Deputy Speaker, Mr Weatherill, in any book on the succession. He has the niceness and lacks the enemies, though his manner can be rather stiff, and Speakers need to have a mild invincibility complex which, considering their semi-Soviet powers of administrative elimination, would be fully justified. Given such assurance a Speaker should be light on his bottom, deftly and humorously settling disputes out of court before anybody has a chance of making a federal case of them. Mr Weatherill is a whit formal and correct, not quite vested with that cunning flippancy which persuades people to behave themselves without their having to be told.

On the opposite extreme, Mr Norman St John-Stevas, whose prospects for the Speakership have been widely talked about, especially by Mr Norman St John-Stevas, has rather more of it than most of us can bear. When for the first time you hear him joke about himself, his cleverness, talent, beauty and general liability to be snatched from us by the angels, it is very amusing. After a while and several more rounds of the same mock-self-mockery Mr Stevas is still around and one begins to feel that the angels know what they are about.

Interestingly, in an office which requires bipartisan consent before appointment, the objections would be coming, not from the Labour side who had a good time during his mildly appalling period as Leader of the House, but from the party to which he belongs.

Other candidates have been mentioned including the high-gloss, black-coated observer of Habsburg Spanish protocol, Mr Edward Du Cann. But Mr Du Cann is somewhat excessively a City man and no one quite wants the Speaker issuing equity stock in the House of Commons. This is a very old-fashioned company.

Clever money is on Mr Mark Carlisle. He had his surprise late run at Education and left on good terms with Mother. He proved surprisingly good in the Commons where he had to cope with Mr Neil Kinnock, the boy Bevan. Homework, good manners, authority, quite a good combination for the Speakership. But wise money is still on Mr Weatherill.

The Commons as an instrument of legislation (if it is really that with so many peremptory powers packed in the Little Minister's Kit by way of statutory instruments, orders and what have you) depends on others besides the Speaker. For a start there are the whips, anonymous characters who adore being told that they function like the three murderers in *Macbeth*. To become a full-time whip is a nice little job these days with lots of prospects. I am watching two amusing and independent men recently appointed from opposite ends of the Tory party, Tristan Garel-Jones and Archie Hamilton, to see whether they remain their agreeable selves or emerge in a few years' time with an aluminium respray and speaking lines like a computer print-out.

Whips take on geographical areas, becoming, say, the North-Western or Welsh whip with specific flocks to bring into their pens at 10 p.m. The risk is always that, like sheepdogs, they may come to have a certain exasperation at the sheep whose eccentricities make them sometimes duck out of the way.

Old-fashioned whips thirty years back knew their place. One does not exactly conjure with the names of Patrick Buchan-Hepburn and William Whiteley. They were hired to keep order, to hit anything that moved and not to aspire beyond an ormolu clock on retirement for themselves. Two things were forbidden them— Ministerial jobs and words. Parliamentary Under-Secretaryships, as most Junior Ministries were called before the great inflation of titles, were reserved for the nattering folk. A whip was like an NCO expecting to give hell on toast to cadets who called you 'sir' for the sweet interim and then to take a pace back and defer to them when their pips came. Yet one remained sedulously influential with these young men as a wise subordinate without expectations. They relied on you for everything. They couldn't do without you and they knew it when it came to handling the ranks, but you were no more going to make Lieutenant-Colonel than Archangel.

At most, in the manner of an honorary commission at the end of long service, you were made Secretary of State for Scotland for a couple of years and collected your viscountcy, which was the political equivalent of a tobacconist's shop. Then something went wrong; Mr Heath became a real Minister with a real Department to boss around and later, due to some failure of will or a hole in the ground elsewhere, he became Prime Minister. Mr Whitelaw took on first the Leadership of the House and then the Home Office; Mr Atkins became Lord Carrington's Vicar on Earth.

On the Labour side, where regimental traditions are better kept and meddling innovation is forcefully resisted, the old ways largely continue. Mr Mellish, a very good Chief Whip, made it all the way to Works, Labour's answer to Scotland. Mr Short alone, in Harold Wilson's imitative phase, acquired a slightly spurious eminence as Deputy Leader, a job which implies sixteenth place in the ratings and the Ministry of Education. But there is very little prospect of Labour's extremely good present Chief Whip, Michael Cocks, coming out as more than a deselected MP. Labour's principle is sound. It acknowledges the distinction between gendarmes and lawmakers. The Tories have set a bad example, despite the great personal virtues of Mr Whitelaw, whom it is now fashionable to shoot down. And one reads with alarm that the Soviet Government, which is closer to the Conservatives (monetary control plus law and order) than either might care to emphasize, has followed in the Tories' wake. The appointment of a head of the KGB as party leader is something we could have warned them against.

Even so whips are something of an anonymous presence. There will always be one sitting on the front bench, saying nothing, indeed barred from utterance give or take the odd one-sentence speech required for certain motions to be put. Incidentally Mrs Thatcher has made few decisions more popular than the promotion of the atrocious, index-finger-jabbing and compulsive Christian, John Selwyn Gummer, to an office conferring on him a silence which one can savour. Though alas the man has now escaped to Employment. Varying the metaphor, they are, in their silent, ever-present fashion, a bit like footmen, something which only the great untaxed of Buckingham Palace can afford these days, but footmen with an outside chance of becoming king.

The other factor in the working of the machine is the Leader of the House. Some people find it a boring job. Mr Whitelaw would sooner become Ambassador to La Paz than go back; other people are just not up to it (Mr St John-Stevas); yet others (the present holder, Mr Biffen, and his predecessor, Mr Pym) are very well suited. When it was given to Mr Michael Foot the results were alarming. Having spent twenty years or more on the back benches abstaining from the corrupting influence of power, he descended, like a pious hermit let loose in Soho. Not since the days preceding Thermidor has the blade descended so often into the lunette of the guillotine. Had the Labour Government continued after 1979 they would have had to move him to somewhere convalescent and soothing like Energy.

The floor-leader, to adopt the American term, must also perform a number of tiresome chores and bits of administrative drudgery. Bills must be deposited in the vote office, major legislation must be sent to Members two clear weekends before the first reading. All very tedious and, if one is busy with the ballet or entertaining the

Queen Mother, altogether intrusive into more civilized activities. This was the undoing of Mr St John-Stevas: for there is a body of barrack-room lawyers, practitioners at the bar of *Erskine May*, who knows by heart every last subclause of that compendium of parliamentary procedure. One thinks of Mr Michael English, one thinks of Mr Robin Maxwell-Hyslop, whose perfect joy it is one damp afternoon in November to discover some error in drafting or some breach of the notifying and depositing rules. In Mr Stevas's short butterfly hour of office Michael English came into his glory. An afternoon hardly ever passed without him being on his feet asking the Speaker, with the Castilian civility of those up to no good, about something which to his horror, Mr Speaker, he had found *not deposited in the vote office*!

The leadership of the House does of course require other qualities than those of a good copying clerk. More than any other Minister, the Leader has to be on tolerable terms with the Opposition who, in a way, are a great part of his department. A thoroughly partisan politician, justly proud of the nice conduct of a broken bottle, would not be the man gently to persuade the Opposition that a debate on their obsession of the month cannot be managed in Government time. Nor would he be suited for that odd little intermezzo called Business Questions, when the floor-leader gets up and reads through a list: Monday—Tomato and Cucumber Board, Consolidated Powers (No. 2) Bill; Tuesday—Defence Estimates; Wednesday—A debate on the Opposition motion deploring the Government's shameless and bloody-handed determination to crush hospital auxiliary workers into a pulp; Thursday—further proceedings on the report stage of the Parish Councils (Miscellaneous Powers) Bill; Friday—Private Members' Business, second reading of the Wild Life Preservation (Members of Aslef) Bill.

On those occasions we have a twenty-minute miniature debate about very nearly anything—an adjournment debate painted by Samuel Cooper. As soon as the Leader of the Opposition has uttered the canonical words, 'I am most grateful to the Honourable Gentleman for the information he has provided', it is open season. Usually the same Leader of the Opposition continues with, 'Can he perhaps tell us why no provision has been made for a debate on Chile?'

Theoretically every questioner wants to know why we are not debating X or, as the case may be, Y. But he knows, the Speaker knows and everyone except the battered public in their gallery knows that Business Questions are the parliamentary equivalent of a legal fiction. Nobody handles this business as well as Mr John Biffen, a very good Leader indeed. He is not rude. He does not make party points, but he does try to keep up interest by some dry, humorous little riposte. This job would be badly done were it in the hands of some specialist in parliamentary plainsong, the sort of politician who reads his brief as if it were divine service. Mr Pym, who has hidden shallows, came quite close to this, splendidly as he tied every last knot and deposited every last Bill. Biffen, who to be candid was not a great success as a Departmental Minister, having too large a share of pessimism to be a good radical, gets the Leader's function almost to perfection. He is adored by the Opposition, even though he appears in their guidebooks under 'here be monsters'. He is not above the drudgery; he is the Labour Party's favourite monetarist and he has precisely that light touch which keeps tempers down. Ideological positions are useless as a guide to a politician's standing with his opponents. In principle Mr Biffen is Atrocity John—'three years' unprecedented austerity'. Yet hardish men from the Labour camp like Mr Eric Heffer collapse into shameless good humour when he is around. By contrast Michael Heseltine, abominator of Thatcher, heavily into compassion, sender of busloads of businessmen around Liverpool, is regarded by the Labour Opposition as a cold-eyed authoritarian with all the human qualities of reinforced concrete.

After the Speaker, the whips and the floor-leader comes the business that preoccupies them. It is the early part of the day, say between 2.30 and 4 p.m., which provides much of the entertaining part of politics. Some people become very stiff and censorious about this happy hour. Question Time, these political scientists will tell you, answers no questions. It has no useful functions and is no part of the serious business of Parliament. Furthermore they will add, in thoughtful pieces for the responsible press, it gives exposure to the showmen and the publicists in Parliament. The truly valuable work of Parliament is done elsewhere, in committee or perhaps in considered contributions made to an audience of four including a chained-up whip at 8.15 p.m.

People who say things like that are either in the Social Democratic Party or should be. Very rarely are they much good as speakers themselves, and at heart they do not care much for anything the chamber does, preferring the candid coalescence of the elect in small, sought-after gatherings. The short, brutal truth is that, though Question Time can sometimes be farcical, Roy Jenkins and people like him can't cope with it.

Questions are not a test of facts but they are a marvellous test of people. This is a fairly free but very secret country in which the people in charge get away with much more than they should. The fair balance between the American habit of persecuting government into paralytic incapacity and the British way of letting government bury its bodies at night has not been found. If the critics of Question Time had it in mind to substitute something which would oblige those set in authority over us to tell more of the truth more of the time I should applaud them. In practice they dislike Question Time because it works as a test of people. It is a link between the public politics of a good vigorous election and the main work of Parliament. It is frequently rough and it is good precisely because it *is* rough. Nobody who minds being shouted at has any business being in politics. There are many button-down souls currently in the House who are either aloof to Question Time or incapable of making a go of it. Discovery of the latter condition usually precedes the former.

People of a Ministerial cast of mind, which is not uncommonly one with a taste for minding other people's business, dislike having to comply with low wretches. But it is good for them. If they have no talent for a good heckle, if they think that the drab, abominable language of a Civil-Service-drafted reply is enough and that supplementary questions are best met with huffy indifference, we get a very good view of them for the snobs of merit they are.

But, somebody may say, surely you may get a good man, a conscientious Minister with a good mind and principles who just doesn't have the necessary talents for a verbal Bonfire Night. Of course, but quiet unflashy talents do have a way of shining through Question Time. I would urge the case of the Chancellor of the Exchequer, Sir Geoffrey Howe. Nothing is going to make him exciting, and he was much mocked for a style which resembled Boycott fifteen runs short of one of his records. But something percolated down—a serious purpose, the courage to take on the riotous element even if he got trampled on, even a quiet niceness which slipped through the street fighting. *Per contra*, Michael Foot, though widely loved personally and for most of his career a bobby-dazzler in debate, has had his defects shown up lately by the chamber and specifically at Question Time. His best friend would not praise him for homework or attention to detail, and the belief that he could ride the parliamentary bike shouting 'Look no research' proved mistaken. He has had the worst of it not just because of Mrs Thatcher's similarities to Peter the Great but also because his own thinness of preparation and lack of detailed grasp kept coming through.

Question Time lasts for an hour each day from Monday to Thursday working its way through a roster of Departments, setting aside the monthly quarter of an hour for such subjects as the subsidized arts, and for that senior back-bencher (at present Mr Arthur Bottomley) doomed to answer for the Commons Service Committee. But two quarter-hours are taken out each week for Questions to the Prime Minister. (Tuesday and Thursday, 3.15 to 3.30 p.m.) The citizen with an inclination to watch the Commons should try to make his visit coincide with these hours. Other things are important but this has the best chance of being interesting. And from 2.30 p.m. the Ministerial team from Government Departments will field questions.

Some of what passes will be aimed at purely local consumption— the Torquay bypass and all its equivalents. Some is undertaken in the line of duty for a trade union or other pressure group. A good example recently which combined both was the repeated questioning by Mr Derek Foster (Lab., Bishop Auckland) who brought up the proposed closure of the Shildon Works of British Rail, which would have put 2,000 people out of work in a town of 14,000. Mr Foster is a mild, unhectoring sort of fellow but he didn't intend the House or the press to forget about his constituents and accordingly the Shildon Works came up like sardines on a limited menu. The decision not to close the Shildon Works was influenced by many factors but a good MP's ability to create not so much hell as a steady recurring ache must have helped.

Other questions are quite forlorn. In 1980 there were relays of demands that something should be done for the textile and carpet industries. They came from both sides of the House with Mr David Trippier (Con., Rossendale) and Mr Robert Cryer (Lab., Keighley) competing with each other in the same doomed cause and asking questions each week about the number of mills closed down in their respective constituencies. Yet even in such sterile deadlock Question Time had some utility. The back-bench Members were asking for a measure of economic protection. The Government believes in free trade. The critics wanted smaller quotas on cheap East Asian imports; this Government, like the last one, is locked into the trade treaty known as the Multi-Fibre Agreement. This requires either to be kept or, if broken, broken discreetly. The Government may have emerged as economic realists and scrupulous observers of international agreements or as the most elevated of mugs. Either way the observer can see and decide.

On a **personal** basis Question Time elevates or diminishes Ministers according to their ability to cope. And it can be the making of a man. The recently elevated Iain Sproat, broadly thought of in polite company as a back-bench brutalist, in his first days as an Under-Secretary at the Department of Trade was tossed an awful ball called the collapse of Laker Airlines. Sproat refused to apologize for what Freddie Laker had stood for and instead went on the attack on behalf of the right to risk and lose as well as win. By choosing to make a fight of it, when he had every excuse for using his brief as a slit trench to disappear into, he overnight turned himself into one of the Government's most effective Junior Ministers and has not paused for breath since.

In speaking of the Laker episode we are moving out of Question Time proper into that recent accretion of the British Constitution, the Ministerial statement. These used to be rare and exceptional things; now we must be averaging about six a week. They are distinguished from personal statements (still a rarity) when a Minister or indeed a Private Member, who by convention may not be challenged, denies allegations that he has had a relationship of an intimate kind with Miss Dolores de Slattern, the widely admired consultant of the East German trade delegation (or alternatively that, these allegations being substantially true, he apologizes for existing and will be seeking the stewardship of the Manor of Northstead). Your more usual statement is Mr Walker explaining the latest stage of a conflict with our 'Community partners' over fish, which has shown all the staying power of *The Mousetrap*. Or it may be the Defence Minister deleting the odd destroyer or purchasing the rocket of the 1990s; or it may be the Prime Minister back from the latest summit of European Prime Ministers with the pieces of concrete hardly out of her handbag.

The statement is read out (and to the rage of some left-wing Members is distributed in the vicious press gallery). The Speaker then makes a rough allocation of time, usually about a quarter of an hour, for questions to be put. Occasionally Mr Thomas, letting the lilt of his *Milk Wood* accent undulate upwards, will say that 'because of the obvious concern among honourable Members he will *quite exceptionally* permit questioning until 4.15'—a full twenty-five minutes.

These sessions, which are in effect particularized extensions of Question Time, are becoming more frequent. It is convenient to let a new decision or disaster, where these can be distinguished, have relatively early exposure. It is even more convenient to work on a time-scale where twenty-five minutes is 'quite exceptional'. No Minister not paralysed with remorse should find it too hard to cope with a short question-and-answer session on a document bearing his name, which he has presumably—at the very least—read.

The very existence of statements and questions is also enormously useful to the whips and the Leader of the House. It is my impression that an ever larger part of parliamentary time is spent on the lawmaking process and that mere debates, arguments between banks of politicians, and not attached to some prospective statute, are diminishing in number. Certainly this seems to be the impression of Mr Michael Foot, whose faith in the efficacy of debate—on anything, from the avoidance of general conflagration to the state of tomato farming—is as absolute as any African villager's attachment to his chicken bones. There can be no doubt about it, debates ward off the 'evil eye'. But your modern administrative politician, with his attention fixed on the statute book, dislikes debates and finds statement-and-question sessions the perfect substitute. The hedonists of the chamber may want word banquets fit for the Caesars, *they* prefer to send out for sandwiches.

Among the odds and ends which make the first hour and a half of the parliamentary day so agreeable to the beaten-down back-bencher are those small devices by which he can get headlines in the *Backwater Star and Argus* and even in the *Daily Mail*. I mean the SO9 (Standing Order No. 9), the point of order and the Ten-Minute Rule Bill. Under the standing orders, which are to the conduct of the House what Queen's Regulations are to the Army, a Member may apply for an emergency debate, providing he lets the Speaker know before noon, if it involves 'a matter of urgent and specific concern'. This all sounds terribly reasonable and open-minded until I recall that in the last three years spent watching the Commons I have seen exactly two emergency debates granted (and one of those after the Opposition front bench had stepped in with a little hint to back up the applicant).

The SO9 is just occasionally used in the forlorn, earnest hope that the Speaker will bend his discretion and authorize the making of time for a three-hour debate either that evening or the next day. In practice it is a short strip of common set aside for the flying of kites. Mr Derek Foster used it to demand a debate over those Shildon workshops. Mr Anthony Marlow who was incensed at the Israeli bombardment of Beirut raised that issue. Mr Tam Dalyell, who was honourably if mistakenly and intemperately opposed to the Falklands operation, used it in the general cause of turning round and going home. Every Northern Member with a factory closing down has used it during this period of depression. Occasionally there is a trifling issue brought up, but in fairness most of these kites are ones which the Members concerned do care for. And the application for the right to debate an issue, if skilfully handled, can be turned into a short stump speech on its merits. This must not be done too crudely as the Speaker periodically intervenes to say, with best Welsh benevolence, 'The Honourable Gentleman must not make the speech he *would* have made if the application were to be granted.' But it is a very cack-handed politician who, required to stress the urgency and specific nature of subject X, cannot actually make the essential points about X in his application. When he has done, in about six or seven minutes, the Speaker recites a form of words: 'The House listened with deep interest/anxious concern to what the Honourable Gentleman had to say. As the House well knows I do not decide what is to be debated, only whether there are grounds for an emergency debate. As the House also knows I am not required to give my reasons for deciding and I regret to say that the matter raised by the Honourable Gentleman does not fall within the scope of Standing Order number nine. Next business.'

The Ten-Minute Rule Bill is a rarer commodity to the daily,

sometimes twice-daily, SO9. It has no chance whatsoever of legislative existence, even less than the Private Members' Bills brought forth on Fridays, a few of which, to ease the frustrated psyche of the back-bench Member, are actually passed into law, usually with a heavy convoy of Government or bipartisan support. The Ten-Minute Bill is either an oration in a good but unhopeful cause or it is a piece of mischief liable to be opposed and a division called over its head.

The only other matter which need detain us before glancing at the main business of the day is the point of order. Rarely, very rarely, a point of order is just that. Some grandmaster of correct form like Mr English, who follows procedure the way other people follow televised snooker, will have discovered a procedural irregularity. In these cases the Speaker listens gravely and promises a ruling the next day which is duly delivered (and is destined for the next edition of *Erskine May* and will thus be of interest strictly to those attracted to this minority cult). Infinitely more often 'point of order' is called out for the purpose of saying something which would itself otherwise be wholly out of order. One Member asked not long ago on a point of order whether he was the only Member to have risen seven times without being called. Mr Thomas murmured something about there having been only one Member who had bobbed up and down seven times.

The point of order is of course invoked in the earnest hope of starting an agreeable fight, especially if something has been said *sotto voce* which the long list of unparliamentary epithets proscribes. Many of these, of the 'miserable cur' sort, are of a ponderous Victorian Gothic kind, but the short primitive epithets of today, the new brutalism of uncivil discourse, are also banned. Such a point of order will be raised in a voice plaintively asking Mr Speaker 'Is it in order for the Honourable Member for Blandings Parva to refer to my Right Honourable Friend as a "fascist-minded gorilla"?', to which sensible Speakers, unless the case is screamingly self-evident, respond by deploring all unparliamentary language and affecting those deficiencies of sight and hearing which are major qualifications for the job.

Points of order may of course come at any time in the day but the main catch is taken roughly between the end of questions and/or statements and the start of principal business. Others made later to a thin, not to say emaciated, House of half a dozen are likely to be constructive and serious and thus of very little interest.

That rest of the day concerns the business of lawmaking. (Though there is the occasional, fixed-term, three-hour debate.) It may be a second reading—that is a broad debate on the general principles of the Bill without the power to amend, or the third or report stages of a Bill where the tidyings up done by the Lords are looked over for ways of untidying them. Above all, there is 'Committee', that state of affairs where the line-by-line minutiae of the Bill under consideration are debated and subjected to amendment, not by a committee kept under seemly wraps upstairs but exposed in all its stupifying dismal grandeur as a 'Committee of the Whole House'. Do not be deceived, tedium is the secret weapon of the executive and great sums have been poured away, splendid futilities undertaken, the Humber Bridge and the Concorde, local government reorganization, decimalization, metrication, increases in VAT and the recent Northern Ireland Assemblies Act have all been brought about through a process laughably supposed to examine and scrutinize but actually functioning to deter and depress all public interest. Since the power of the whips is grotesque, the ability of the Private Member to stop a law, even to amend it, is so nearly zero that the pretences to scrutiny of the committee stage on a Bill are essentially fraudulent.

Even filibustering is a ritual. There is almost a convention, in the full constitutional sense of the term, governing how long the rococo art of time-wasting can be spun out before the inevitable timetable motion is introduced. The attitude of the Minister and his whips in the early stages of a filibuster is that of Thomas Gray contemplating the children of his old school, 'Alas, regardless of their doom, the little victims play'. Those tempted to take the House of Commons too seriously should recall that a great deal of it is about 'play', or at best occupational therapy. Unless and until you can get office and want to use it, life is a delightful adventure playground, periodically interrupted by whips telling you which door to go through. Mr Enoch Powell is an exception, but Mr Powell is an exception to everything.

Understandably the general public, coming into their gallery and watching this process of simulation, are perplexed. Perhaps they have stumbled in upon the private game of space invaders played by Social Democrats and Hooligans on the front bench below the gangway, or alternatively if they are really unlucky, they may hear some virtuoso of verbal drabness like Mr Geoffrey Finsberg or Sir Michael Havers answer questions. Worst of all they may alight upon the House in committee, the mace reverently removed, the Chairman of Ways and Means in the chair (never the Speaker) and somebody drawing the attention of all fifteen Honourable Members present to the villainous iniquity of clause four, line three. (By the way, Members absenting themselves from these sessions are not neglecting their duties, just understanding them.)

The public generally looks slightly stupefied, not least the crocodiles of children and the Foreign Office batch of Nigerians in tribal costume brought in to observe 'the way our Parliament works'. The purpose of this book is not to spend long enlightening that perplexity by explaining or rationalizing the parliamentary process but to acknowledge that Parliament is a place where power is put on display in the persons of those holding it, a testing ground where power may be achieved by hungry infantry, who look beseechingly upwards. It may be lost there by an individual's showing too extravagant an ineptitude, though parliamentary incapacity is all too slight a bar to success. And it may be glowered at in retrospective resentment by those who had it but have it no more.

What is most interesting about the Commons is the group of people to be found in it; the personality of the men seeking authority is the least trivial subject imaginable. At their most meritable they are entertaining. If they are dull it is useful to know as much. History is made, not only by Cleopatra's nose but by Anthony Eden's bile duct. I shall write about these people and their personalities, as holders, potential holders or past holders of power, indicating how they perform and where I think they are going. The place is after all a great club where everybody knows everybody else even if only for the purpose of mutual loathing. There are no people on earth so apt as MPs at marking each other's cards to a third party. Partly, this is because they are in a combative game and are thus as knowledgeable as thin-faced Irishmen in pork-pie hats on Lambourn Downs on the topic of form and, very often, of breeding.

2

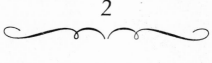

Exodus, Kings and
Revelations

The Labour Party with its passion for elections (though not just at present for a general election) has always elected its principal front-bench spokesmen. Now this is one of the few pleasures of life still afforded to Labour MPs, a melancholy body of men who do not even, like the Quakers, divide into Plain and Gay, but show a generally morose condition.

It is a rotten thing to be a Labour MP today. Go to Party Conference and you will see them sitting on their own stand, not as a mark of respect but as a collective form of what the Scottish Kirk used to call 'the stool of penitence', like so many seventeenth-century adulterers in Arbroath. Actually any Labour MP who does manage a little light adultery thoroughly deserves it. There are zealots waiting in the body of the hall to point contemptuously at the 'class traitors', 'enemies of the working class', 'Westminster scabs', and 'them'. If the individual MP speaks, he can choose between being brave and the abuse which goes with that, or sycophantically militant, with the indifferent tolerance which that can buy. One does not have to admire the Social Democrats to see why they exist. Mr Neville Sandelson put it well when just before his *last* Conference he applied instead for his first ever parliamentary free trip as part of a delegation visiting Gibraltar. 'The company of the apes', said Mr Sandelson, 'would be such a relief.'

Accordingly, the Parliamentary Party, which is still right-wing Labour, makes the most of its diminished powers and chooses a shadow cabinet reflecting its tastes. The beseeching heights of the

Opposition front bench are still occupied by renegades, opportunists, objective class enemies and men of talent.

Actually it is a surprisingly good front bench, though the twenty-year domination of senior Labour politicians over their Tory equivalents is no longer evident. But the decline has largely been one of will-power, nerve and political faith. Partly through their own fault in the complacent, coasting past, the men who lead Labour now do so on a manifesto in the greater part of which they disbelieve, commanding parliamentary colleagues caught between the devil of de-selection and the deep beige sea of Social Democracy. Their opposition to Norman Tebbit's Trade Union Bill, which would have had them swinging from the microphones ten years ago, was like the interlude ballet in the old French opera, something for which nobody had any real enthusiasm but which had to be kept up as a long-standing tradition of the company. On defence, poor Mr Silkin, a man with a lot of enemies, has to strike a balance between the unilateralism to which he is lashed and his own regard for the defence of the country.

On employment and industrial matters Labour spokesmen who, with three million unemployed, should have turned the Commons into a lido of happy rage, find instead that the depression affecting business has spread remorselessly to the Labour benches. Destocking has taken place on an alarming scale, turnover is low and many shop windows are boarded up. But if trade is list-less, if the never-to-be-matched circumstances of three million unemployed do not find the Opposition in the unpleasing exaltation of politicians within sight of office, it is not the fault of individual talent.

Mr Foot's shadow Ministers are very capable, usually more nimble than the corresponding Conservative, less reliant on the set words in the brief—the mechanical, drab devotion which fills so much space on the Government side especially among the older Junior Ministers. Yet Labour spokesmen at present persistently fall below those abilities.

Why, for example, does Mr John Silkin essentially fail? For a start he is in the wrong job, Defence, having been in another wrong job, Industry. He is clever and, despite a real flair for unpopularity, extremely nice. Jewish, kindly, rather overweight, he is not at heart a partisan politician. For the issue on which Silkin scored and scored again, something registered by the deep loathing which the other side took to him, was the Common Market. In that intervening period before the full levy of the Budget hit us, when John Silkin dealt with Agriculture as a Minister, he was, if only in parliamentary terms, hugely effective. He held strong and violent convictions which gave him impetus in argument and created the impression of a man moving irresistibly upwards. As recently as thirty months ago the ultimate leadership (after whatever Foot or Healey interim might intervene) was thought to be a race between Shore and Silkin. Mr Shore is still a very serious candidate. For Mr Silkin, regretfully, I think it can't happen. As shadow Minister of Industry facing Sir Keith Joseph, he became slightly liturgical. Conscientious but not passionate, he tended to put a spurt of shock and horror into the last paragraphs of his speeches, as if the peroration had been marked on the score with four *f*s. But he is desperately unsuited to shouting at people or at punching dispatch boxes. Noisily insincere people like Mr Peter Walker do that sort of thing so much better.

At Defence he is, of course, in an even worse position. The Party has effectively gone unilateralist and the job which is the equivalent in terms of rank-and-file popularity to being Minister for Nationalization in a Conservative Government, has become impossible. Mr Silkin is in a false position, obliged to function like Polyfilla in a very nasty crack in the Party's façade. Not being a false man, just an ordinarily pragmatic and compliant fellow, he looks like Hilaire Belloc's definition of the middle class— 'underdone and harassed, out of place and mean and horribly embarrassed'. (Though 'mean' would be the most unjust adjective imaginable for him.)

He was also, without getting the credit for it, distinctly brave in putting up a dummy candidacy for the 1981 deputy leadership election—the one resolved at the great hate-in at Brighton. That candidacy was appreciated by the Bright Left, which sometimes seems to be confined to Mr Michael Meacher, for what it was—a raft for the rescue of all those whose past romanticism or career-leftism had put them into the Tribune Group, but whose understanding of political gravity left them appalled at the notion of Mr Wedgwood Benn as the chief lion beneath the throne.

Something else is well worth remembering, not least because, having happened in the 1960s, it pre-dates political memory. Silkin, untypically for the Labour Party, rose from the post of Chief Whip. Now the tradition of Labour Chief Whips is that they are on the Right of the Party and expect to be obeyed. Silkin succeeded Ted Short, not exactly Carlos the Jackal, but a fairly hard case from the Geordie Mafia who had been a headmaster, had a parliamentary majority of four to work on and gave his orders smartly. Silkin, by contrast, inherited both Harold Wilson's hundred majority and Harold Wilson's ultimately disastrous desire to be nice to people. Silkin was glad to oblige, and his period as Chief Whip was praised for its reasonableness, good nature, common sense and tolerance.

Perhaps this was partially a reflection of Harold Wilson's own rather tragic combination of kindness and weakness. But Chief Whip is not a natural job for pleasant men; yet pleasantness evidently showed and it undoubtedly helped the subsequent stages of Silkin's career. But it is interesting to see what happens when the office is not held by a South American army interrogator. You get risings in the hills.

Silkin today, like so many of his colleagues, seems to be operating on half his cylinders. The work is done, the facts are known, but there is not enough passion to light a match. He is also in the position of being notionally on the Left of the Party, something remaining from an earlier definition of 'Left'. Tribune membership has so often been taken out by men of temperate views as a sort of insurance policy, a pinch of incense to Jupiter implying no very devout convictions.

His colleague Neil Kinnock has some affinities with Silkin, but not ones that should be pushed too far. Miss Joan Maynard, one of Parliament's most notable admirers of the Soviet system, who, with her hair done up behind and her glinting glasses, irresistibly suggests one of those female Russian judges liable to send you down on a renewable sentence, once remarked of Mr Kinnock, 'I'm very worried about Neil. I'm afraid that he might do a Stan Orme.' It was a shrewd comment. Like the well-loved member for Salford East, Mr Kinnock has had his period of fervid, technicolour left-wingery, but like Stan Orme he is influenced by membership of the human race. He is also both Welsh and intelligent, a combination which obliges anyone so endowed to start looking over his shoulder at Aneurin Bevan and Lloyd George. It also usually implies a facility which will be called mastery, a cleverness which will be called wizardry and, when it comes to words, a certain velocity of circulation. He has a good deal to drive him on. Like so very few in politics he is the genuine child of the working class, come up through University (Cardiff) and he has a delightful wife with ambitions for her husband which are surpassed only by Lady Howe and the voluble Mrs Prior.

On top of that he truly can talk well. His jokes are excellent, like the prophetic comment on Mr Jenkins long ago: 'Roy was canvassing at a working-class household and was turned away in a kindly way—"No, sorry boy. We're Labour here."' He is even a nice man with the gift of being liked by the Tories without compromising his views. He *has* of course modified them, but for less futile purposes than pleasing the Conservatives.

One would not want to confuse Neil Kinnock's rational mellowing with the champagne decadence which marked Aneurin Bevan well before the end. He is not precisely an operator and the Left of today with its whiff of black leather and street coercion is, anyway, one that can be honourably set at several miles' distance by those who still believe in their own radicalism. First into the shadow cabinet at 37, a majority of 20,000, and now talked about perfectly seriously, although he has never held ministerial office, as a candidate for the succession to Mr Foot, Kinnock is a politician's dream . . . about himself.

And yet (and there is a fair measure of 'and yet' about him), Kinnock is showing signs, now that he is at the top, of not being quite able to cope. With such a brilliant start he may yet be the Labour Party's answer to the composer Mascagni, who said of himself, after the triumphs of his first opera had been followed by a sad succession of faint praise and downright failure, 'I was crowned before I was king.' Kinnock has a lovely gift of wit and fluency just as the composeer of *Cavalleria Rusticana* had a lovely gift of melody, but he tends to skate over boring difficulties and the horse work of getting his facts right. It was said of Mascagni that he was too ready to settle for his first drafts. This perfectly describes the small ginger Welshman whose best speeches are a triumph of inspiration over absent homework.

This was illustrated when Kinnock was in regular debate with the former Education Minister, Mark Carlisle. To stand by the musical metaphor, Carlisle is like one of those teachers of strict counterpoint who have never felt like whistling, and he took Kinnock, tenderly and apologetically, apart. The House would get first the complete, Welsh grandeur of the eloquence boyo bit—torrents coming down from Cader Idris, adjectives dancing in the stream like trout, a flood of glittering indignation cascading down in a way which should have carried the Minister away. Instead Carlisle would ask, in his quietest voice, a polite question. The debate had been about the alleged shortage of textbooks, the Honourable Gentleman was alleging that in some areas schools were reduced to raffling these books. That was a most serious matter, but would the Honourable Gentleman please tell him where and in which schools this had taken place? What followed could unkindly be called orator's block, a long pause accompanied by agitated movements. Mr Kinnock then muttered something about 'well-known facts'. And, as suddenly, Cader Idris was made to look a little like a stage set for *The Maid of the Mountains*.

However, a reformed Kinnock, if he can kick some of his gaudier habits and develop a modified passion for detail, would be something to keep the Tories awake at nights. He is a likeable man with a sense of humour, unlikely qualities in a politician; and uncommonly for a shortish radical he lacks malice. Incidentally a lot of late Mascagni was by no means bad: and the people who know about these things say that the finest opera he ever wrote was the seldom performed *Il Piccolo Marat*. Think on.

The landscape changes when one moves on the Labour front bench from Education to Employment, not an easy progression these days. Eric Varley has little in common with Neil Kinnock except the remnants of reddish hair. As a Minister he had an alarming habit of being both correct in his judgements and overruled in cabinet. Varley wanted to close the hopeless Linwood car factory which made a loss in eighteen of the nineteen years of its existence. Terror at what then looked like the inexorable advance of Scottish Nationalism led to the Scottish Secretary, Mr Ross, and the Labour Party's man of affairs, Mr Harold Lever, demanding that money should be forwarded gratefully, regardless of loss. Mr Varley, the least hard-hearted of men, advised against the operation in the naïve belief that even non-commercial funding with a social purpose should be based on some hope of turning the enterprise in the vague direction of solvency. Nobody had introduced Mr Varley to Dr Maurice Cowling of Cambridge who has constructed a complex political theory which states that nothing, absolutely nothing, is ever done except for low motives, commonly to win by-elections.

Perhaps he was learning from Dr Cowling when he set up the De Lorean factory in Belfast; certainly he had not gauged the depth of Mr De Lorean's motives, something worth thinking about.

If any of this makes Eric Varley look like a fool it is not intended to. He is one of the most admirable politicians in the Commons. He is entirely honest within the possibilities of the game and is as near as one can get to the authentic seam of the English working class anywhere near the top of politics. The son of a miner, and himself a skilled craftsman, he never plays the stage proletarian.

He had his own teenage phase of being a 'dangerous extremist', but such attitudes are not natural to his temperament. Interestingly, although he was specifically appointed to the Industry Ministry by Harold Wilson as a sobering agent after Tony Benn's great carouse there he is never reproached for his present position in the spectrum. No one confuses him with the clareteers. He has patrial feelings towards the Labour Party and once said that if the unbearable people took over, he would not join Another Organization, would not even make the sort of fuss which keeps the Tory press in headlines. 'I would just quietly get up and walk away'. Eric Varley, owing vast amounts to the Labour Party, remembers the fact and stays with it even in a time of apparently irreversible decline. Although he fits better than anyone the idea of the educated industrial worker whom people like Attlee saw as the heirs of an earlier necessary paternalism, he will not be leader.

He has the reverse defects of integrity, a certain shortage of the dazzle factor, a tendency to be Richardson to somebody else's Olivier (though we have had some truly terrible Oliviers). He is also unlucky in his present job. It puts him opposite Norman Tebbit, which is like getting yourself in a trench against the Death's Head Hussars. And Varley is using, as he perhaps now realizes, all the wrong weapons. Conditioned by Tebbit's cannibalistic guerrilla warfare on the back benches he spent a lot of time denouncing, treating the Minister as if he had stepped out of a double-X-certificated film with hair on the backs of his hands, making low brutish noises.

The visitors' gallery was once badly thrown to hear a dialogue in which the Opposition spokesman called the Minister a disgrace and, effectively, a marginal member of the human race, only to have Mr Tebbit say that he was, as a naturally moderate man, rather hurt that Mr Varley should be so intemperate. It was like setting an elephant trap and seeing a gazelle walk over it.

Eric Varley is the Labour Party's Treasurer, a position from which leaderships were once won, but now an annual ordeal by Delegate Conference. In taking up the challenge of contesting the post in 1981 he was opposing Norman Atkinson, a deeply unengaging political primitive. It was a good victory, perhaps evidence of some movement from the ultra Left among trade unionists, or more likely Terry Duffy at last turning his AUEW majority into a vote he could deliver.

A front-bencher who, physically at least, fits the notion of an absent-minded piece of Gothic fantasy, is Mr Gerald Kaufman. It seems almost no time at all since Mr Joe Haines, immortalizing life in the back pantry under Harold Wilson, described how he threw something across the office at the head of an understrapper's mate called Kaufman with the succinct comment, 'Creep.' Most of us would have regarded Sir Harold's press officer as having delivered all the comment that would ever be called for. But we were quite wrong. It is only part of the truth. Most back-room functionaries who go on into politics from the leader's private office bring a debilitating discretion with them, a dun-coloured personality or no personality at all. One thinks, but not for long, of Mr Tom McNally.

Kaufman was not like this at all. Not only was he rapidly promoted (itself proof of nothing), but he began to flash and glitter, to say, or more often write, witty and explosive things, and, long before his fiftieth year, he had been elected to the shadow cabinet. Now since this is what sociologists call peer-group selection, it cannot be achieved by ingratiating or creeping except of a very broad-cast, widely directed sort. The real reasons were that he had both competence as a speaker and a sense of humour. In his book, *How to be a Minister*, he was agreeably disrespectful: 'The Labour Government had no idea what a planning agreement, the corner-stone of its policies, was.' 'When being interviewed on TV do not allow yourself to be disturbed by such irrelevancies as the actual question asked.' And perhaps pre-emptively: 'Some Prime Ministers warm to the genuine and dedicated sycophant.'

It was an impudent and unpompous book which candidly admitted the pure pleasure of being looked after by one's own sycophants, having a large official car and someone to drive it, the little things which invest Ministers with at first unease, then masterful assurance and, on termination, feelings of desolation. All titular heads of anything, from the nation to a subsection of the Department of the Environment, are pampered, both physically and emotionally. Nothing is quite so bitter-sweet as the sound of a Minister telling other people 'to live in the real world', when he has a return ticket to the Edwardian upper class in his coat pocket. It was great honesty in Gerald Kaufman to have admitted as much, and to have sent himself up so elegantly.

Yet, for a wit, he spends a good deal of his time on the front bench making chunteringly indignant speeches of a kind he surely cannot take seriously himself. And indeed when he was a Minister (number three at Industry) there were some involuntarily self-satirical moments: 'Any trade union leader has only to lift his telephone and I will see him.' (Group sycophancy perhaps.)

This may explain the passion with which Kaufman hurls himself against the Secretary of State for the Environment (as the Minister of Local Government and Works is heavily known). Kaufman has variously described Michael Heseltine as 'the enemy of local government', 'the South Oxfordshire looter', 'guilty of criminal frivolity' and 'the commissar of local government'. One does not quarrel with the substance of this, but the style is too heavy and closer to the dull norm of Labour Party atrocity-fancying than one would have hoped for from a man who said that, as a Minister, 'your final paragraph should be grandiloquent, almost meaningless'. Also, we could have done without the denunciation of cricketers playing sinfully for money in South Africa as 'having their hands covered with blood-soaked kruggerands'. He was not helped by the presence at that very moment of the shadow Minister of Sport at a celebration thrown by Soviet sporting authorities on the Black Sea in the sort of blood-soaked comfort never very far from the ministerial class even *out* of office.

Still one complains only in moderation. No one can be against Michael Heseltine and be all bad. The present Minister has given Labour spokesmen a chance to look like libertarians if they cared to and it is a less alien stance for Gerald Kaufman than many. His commitment to the substitution of local income tax in place of rates is probably wrong for a lot of technical reasons, but it was at least an initiative. Again it is soothing to hear a Labour spokesman talking about one-tier local government. Though how much more soothing it would be not to hear any spokesman talking about local government at all.

Kaufman's image outside Westminster is still that of a slick, slight hanger-on, accidentally hoisted up. That is simply wrong. He is not going to lead the party (if in five years' time anyone in his senses still *wants* to) but he is a major reinforcement to the moderate wing, in whose cause he grows increasingly partisan. Bald, glinting, slightly built, a little stooped, he looks like a creep. Probably he once was a creep. But we should not over-stress the past. Edward Heath was once editor of the *Church Times*. After the misfortunes of Dr David Owen no one is going to be called 'outstandingly able' again for some time. Let us settle for 'pretty damn good'.

One turns to the Opposition spokesman on Transport with anxiety. Mr Albert Booth, Member for Barrow-in-Furness, has been the object of so much random derision that good taste alone urges that one should stay one's hand. Still, we must not let good taste run away with us. Mr Booth is the sort of politician who as a parliamentary Under-Secretary would not have been noticed. On promotion to the last Labour cabinet, he was in regular receipt of the sort of notices which Eduard Hanslick gave to Wagner, without the consolation of being Wagner, so he must sometimes have regretted the elevation. He owed it entirely to Michael Foot, whose deputy and then successor he was at Employment.

He belongs politically on the old Soft Left, uncritical of anything a trade union might do even if it passed a resolution to follow the correct line taken by Brother Herod. He gave a display of this during the Aslef strike of July 1982, when the shared attitude of Mr Foot and himself brought from Sydney Weighell the observation 'We're not very happy about you and Albert.' A pro-Aslef line was not left-wing any more than it was good politics. It represented for both men a twitch of involuntary loyalty—conditioned and unconditional. Calculation would have said that there were more NUR members (paying more to Party funds) than there were people sitting in the sidings with Mr Buckton's executive. While supporting Aslef has a distinct edge over supporting Argentina, it is not the sort of attitude the attentive politician should be seen adopting. But Aslef is a trade union and it was on strike, and to Albert Booth must thus have been essentially in the right. There are more purely class attitudes in politics than are acknowledged. While Michael Foot would be paying homage to an adopted class it would never cross Albert Booth's mind—not a long journey— to be anything but loyal to any workers in dispute. He is all too evidently (whatever virtue there may be in such attitudes) the rank and file established in office. He is upright, he is hard-working, and he is profoundly honourable, as such disastrous judgements show.

As a parliamentarian he has a pedestrian, deliberate manner suggesting a policeman of the older school proceeding in an orderly fashion. But without being unkind, I think he is boxing above his weight; and, more seriously, he is perhaps the most acute case of purely corporate thinking on the Labour front bench, the sort of man whose loyalty and honourable feelings towards his group make him a delegate before he is a representative.

Mr Booth's speeches always sound as if some particularly eloquent statue had come to the dispatch box. Even the fact that the statue speaks with the most beautiful accent of the English tongue, that of Northumberland, doesn't make it much easier to live with. Although Albert Booth belongs strictly within the democratic Labour tradition, his narrow, inflexible style is reminiscent of what it must be like having to listen to the Second Secretary of the Slovakian Central Committee on a particularly trying day in Bratislava.

In Peter Shore Labour has a strange character. Seven years ago the Tory press uncomprehendingly linked opposition to the Common Market Referendum to the well-known soul brothers of the Left, 'Benn and Shore'. Conservative politicians used them in unison much as little girls will hang pairs of cherries over their ears. In consequence Peter Shore, who in shadow cabinet made it his business to confront to the death the details of theoretical assertions made by Benn, and to win the arguments, was cloudily identified as the leftist he has never been. Shore, who has an old-fashioned English regard for England and a bottomless contempt for the Soviet system, and who is neither an enemy of private business nor a cheer-leader for the unions, somehow got the name of being a sort of candidate member of the Committee of Public Safety.

It was all very funny and did him no harm whatsoever. He obtained all the benefits of trimming without ever having trimmed. By reason of his attacks on the Common Market he had moved from being an unexciting occupant of office with a jittery delivery to the standing of a cottage Cromwell.

So many politicians proclaim their passionate care for a subject that the word and the notion die in the air as forms of fraudulence too transparent to have been worth trying on. 'Rodney cares passionately about Europe' was the sort of phrase, much in circulation in the late sixties. Today it has all the standing of a rolled-gold krugerrand and Rodney is caring passionately about the inner-city areas. The distinguishing thing about Shore is that he *was* passionate as an enemy of the EEC. A frail, bony man whose nose and front hair seem to have made a *coup d'état* for the control of his face, he tore into the whole idea with a force which seemed likely to make him disintegrate. He was funny and sarcastic and carried details in belts of machine-gun ammunition.

Shore, whose antecedents were vague in most people's minds, passed as a left-winger for want of any attempt to identify his thinking. In fact, like Gerald Kaufman, he owed his career to Sir Harold Wilson and was described about ten years ago as *Homo wilsonicus*.* Shore in his early days was a poor speaker and much derided as the gross over-promotion of the office intellectual who clearly had no parliamentary talent.

The EEC not only gave him credit with the Left and general prominence, it also struck a vein of fire, irony and platform force on which he can still draw. Precisely because he is attracted to ideas his quality as a speaker tends to improve where that of an opportunistic orator becomes rapidly exhausted and repetitious. A golden tongue wears very thin.

Even so Shore's rating is probably lower as a speaker than it should be. Old reputations are only gradually shrugged off and he does occasionally become a trifle donnish. This though can lead to delightful put-downs as on the occasion when the Government had retreated from a plan to cut down overseas broadcasts, but had economized instead on the booster station intended to maintain effective transmission. 'Nation shall murmur unto nation,' said Mr Shore. For this, as well as splendidly raging and contemptuous speeches on the economy, he is standing well to the front of the Party for the day when the election of a new leader comes. Whether he is actually helped by the close affection and understanding between him and Mr Foot is a nice point. But it symbolizes the comfortable coexistence which now exists between the Soft Left—Foot, Stan Orme, Albert Booth, John Silkin—and the anti-Common Market Right—Douglas Jay, Peter Shore, Eric Varley.

Shore has, characteristically, been direct and intellectually consistent in his loathing of the 'Oi' element now practising that barbarous noun formation, 'entryism'. The Labour Party has had more trouble with that even than the Palace. There have been occasions when he has functioned as Mr Foot's hit man, going down into the roughest quarters of politics to call the Militant Tendency a conspiracy and to put aside all the little mantras about the wrongness of witch hunts and divisive attitudes. During the Falklands war he had a considerable influence in allying his own English patriotism with the instinct of others not to wire themselves up to the mains by opposing the Task Force. As an economics spokesman he did not speak directly on the subject, but he supported the action strenuously and helped Mr Foot minimize any urge to see it as Suez redivivus. If he could have got his word in more quickly he would also have hauled his leader back from

---

* Most politicians at the top gather small courts around them—Heathmen, Gaitskellites, FORJ (the Friends of Roy Jenkins)—but Sir Harold did not. The misfortunes of Sir Harold's *private* personal circle, whether active in the slag-heap conversion business or helping the police in their enquiries, has been dwelt on enough. He should be given credit for the fact that the two politicians who have emerged through his close favour, Gerald Kaufman and Peter Shore, have been as talented and substantial as they come.

supporting Aslef, one of the higher forms of self-immolation.

I have this feeling that Shore may be the next leader of the Party. It is a chancey thing to say that with Denis Winston Healey on the open veld and the Far Left in the undergrowth. But (the God who occasionally takes politicians away permitting) the next election is going to be between Tony Benn and the man with the best chance of beating him. Shore, by contrast, without ever having crept, has followed what seemed like a strange trail of his own, single-minded antipathy to the Common Market and consequential dislike of the SDP, old-fashioned (now very new-fashioned) patriotism, and disdain for the Soviet system; on top of which, in his abstracted way, Shore is quite nice to people. The fools whom Mr Healey doesn't suffer gladly he regards as adhering to a fallacy which should be explained to them.

It is very little, perhaps not at all, calculated, but as a formula for achieving broad toleration it works. There will be confraternal blocs in Parliament of Left–Shore supporters and Right–Shore supporters who meet in a strange confluence of the Crosland tradition and the Foot tradition. Those unions concerned to stop Tony Benn will support the candidate best able to do it. If you were Terry Duffy or Frank Chapple you would be preoccupied with dropping pieces of concrete on Mr Benn. If Healey's age and the old enmities he has in Parliament stop him from gathering the maximum anti-Benn parliamentary vote, those union leaders in close liaison with the PLP will settle for the man who can stop the enemy. It is an old Labour tradition.

Denis Healey himself is something special. The first recorded occasion on which he was described as a lone wolf was in 1957. He has never belonged to anybody's admiration group and had no more than associate membership of the Gaitskellites; he was at a notable distance from the Cult of Roy which always reminds one of those cash-and-carry Indian mystic groups, the advertisements for whose perfect master are everywhere to be seen on the London Underground. His relationship with the Left is best summed up by the occasion when, after some heckling by Mr Canavan, Healey completed his speech, walked towards the exit, bowed to the Speaker from the Bar of the House and then stood over Canavan, and said repeatedly 'You short crisp obscenity.'

The only person in the House who compares with him for intelligence is Enoch Powell—both, oddly, are classicists and Italian-speakers. He has a cultivation of mind and an appetite for books, pictures and music which is wolfish. At the same time he gets a good deal of pleasure from being considered a low sort of fellow. He has better and more expensive tastes in wine than Mr Jenkins, but no one would dream of using the claret jibe against him. He is a great deal better versed, I suspect, in the literature of

Europe than Mr Jenkins, with an interesting enthusiasm for the
prose of Heine, but he has never confused a continental culture
with the EEC. He is in the tradition of the muscular intellectual, like
the sort of Victorian who could quote Propertius and lay out a
passing ruffian with his Penang Lawyer. He admires Mrs Thatcher's
intestines but not her mind. He is probably the most delightful
Member of the House actually to talk with. If he does not become
leader (as I fear, will be the case) one does not expect a sour, self-
justifying presence petulantly flapping at a prepared text on his
knee to tell the Speaker that a Privy Councillor is invoking his
precedence to make some petty oration which will compare the
present terrible state of things with the time 'when I, Mr Speaker,
was Lord High Whatever'. He has access to things more interesting
than his injustices. There is a fair old ego there, but it is exercised
daily in healthy unarmed combat. Should you meet Mr Healey, do
not dispute too seriously with him, he may jump on your windpipe.

He has in fact a high-powered normality with nothing of the prig,
no more than is absolutely necessary of the responsible statesman,
quite a lot of the cynic, a negligible element of the self-pity which
afflicts the trade and quite a measure of the roughneck. This last is
held against him by people with tight mouths and rimless spectacles
who tend to murmur the word 'thug', as if we were not sadly short
of the high-quality version of that article.

So what is wrong? Healey has, after all, enormous seniority yet he
is actually doing for Mr Foot precisely the job, shadow Foreign
Secretary, to which he was appointed by Hugh Gaitskell in 1956. He
was defeated for the leadership partly because half a dozen votes
were cast by future members of the SDP on the principle that things
would have to get worse before they could get better. Accordingly,
a final six inches were added to the parapet of credibility. He has
behaved well in defeat. He always behaves well in essentials. But
his defeat may also have roots in his outsiderism. While he wants
office, enjoys it and puts on periodic spurts of dues-paying
conformity, his actual gifts work against him politically. He can and
will try to please; he can and does play below his own alpha level,
but he makes a terrible job of it.

There is a certain kind of blustering Healey speech made to please
the Party's groundlings which depresses his admirers and which
reminds one of an Irishman making his point by hitting somebody
over the head with a bucket. Healey speaks a number of foreign
languages well, but his grasp of primitive Labour rhetoric is very
rusty. Too generous to be an élitist, too sophisticated to be a
populist, he slips between the options. If he regularly gave us the
best of himself he might just be unbeatable. So often the Labour and
Conservative Parties in Parliament remind me of two teams, one
each from the old third division North and third South. A class

player can make a transforming difference or he can fall in with the norm and boot the ball upfield with vigorous indifference and be applauded for his forcefulness.

There is another important fault. Like a number of physically brave men, he has a streak of timidity or, if you like, of passivity in the face of bad developments. He has better intellectual equipment than Peter Shore (better than most people for that matter) but it was Shore who bothered to fight out the issues with Tony Benn in the National Executive. Healey, who has a huge contempt for most of the Left, has engaged on occasions, but he seems at times to have learned, against his own nature, from the optimistic inertia of Harold Wilson. He has perhaps too much faith that when the drums and thunder are past things will be much as they were before, hardly the experience of the Labour Party in the last decade.

How one would feel about the loss of Roy Hattersley is another matter. Hattersley's loyalty seems to be on castors: 'May I explain to you, Tony, why I feel I must vote for Jim?' 'No. Fuck off.'

His opportunism was so magnificent that one struggles for comparisons—a Yorkshire Gonzaga, as trustworthy as Francis Pym but much nicer, Harold Wilson improved by Colley Cibber; one can never do justice to Hattersley. Hattersley is the sort of person for whom the word 'engaging', used ruefully, seems to have been custom-built. When he is shocked, he is noisily shocked. There is certainly a sense of humour but, unlike most politicians so handicapped, he takes nothing lightly. Indeed perhaps his failure to deviate is from a sense of the enormous seriousness of the game.

In debate he does well enough but never quite managed the demolition job one had hoped for on Michael Heseltine. Hattersley is fluent in the Labour Party rhetoric which Healey so stumbles over. Indeed he seems to be bilingual in the temperate argued discussion and the sort of invective which would receive wide expression if the *Daily Mail* were a Labour paper.

Will he go far, this arm-chancing Denry Machin? Well, among the shadows he has gone a long way already—shadow Home Secretary, a post taken from the mild, uncombative Merlyn Rees, is plenty of seniority to be going on with. His name is of course mentioned in connection with the next leadership election and he will stand. But my dispassionate guess is that he might get a humiliatingly small vote, not from unpopularity but because the next election will be a deadly serious business, a sectarian one. Hattersley for all his talents is a superb light-comedy actor and we are casting *King Lear*. He is also somewhat screamingly in the mould of Sir Harold, beer and sandwiches and a bad bargain at 3 in the morning. All things to all men is very useful but not after the point where you become nothing very definite to anybody.

Hattersley is shrewd. As the trends go he is Seismic Man. The term Social Democrat, though we forget the fact, had been used for a number of years before the creation of a separate party, broadly to describe that wing of the Labour Party which finds the word 'Right' too naked and 'moderate', too rubberily inexact. Well before the schism and the launching of the new party Hattersley was going around redefining himself . . . as a democratic socialist. By lashing himself to the Labour Party's withered mast he claims to be showing loyalty to the Party of his fathers. I would sooner give him credit for having got his long-term calculations about the prospect of any breakaway group exactly right.

Hattersley, who does not give the impression of being disinterested but whose self-interest is at least decently on display, was too shrewd to join the SDP, and not credibly able to join anything more seaworthy. Accordingly he has a deep and abiding loyalty to the Labour Party. If things go really badly, he has, like Birmingham, the city which he enthusiastically represents, considerable talent for diversification. The journalism he did, first for the weeklies, was not the work of a good amateur. He may end up as the highly successful editor of a national newspaper. It's better than playing Philadelphia.

One finds with some surprise, having run through a clutch of front-bench Labour politicians—and it has to be incomplete: Stan Orme, Merlyn Rees and of course Mr Foot will be appearing elsewhere—that dislike has loomed so small. Broadly this is a bunch of likeable, capable, moderate men. Yet there are instances of pure poison on the Government bench.

This attractiveness may simply be a by-product of failure. Labour has undergone a near martyrdom at the hands of its dreadful and devouring youth—seventeenth-century millenarians taught by people who once read a book about Althusser, dude proletarians like Mr Scargill's bus-borne squadristi. The Party is nagged and blackguarded by a Conference from which the spirit of good nature has drained away. The misfortunes may be partly the consequence of their own complacency and unwillingness to speak out in the past, but those misfortunes have left the front bench with some of the qualities of Job, and have actually thrown them together. The Labour Party is split all right, into alpha and omega factions who belong to different cultures, different civilizations; but the front bench is not. Those who sit there are laggard in the mutual knife-work which distinguishes most groups of ambitious men. The odd grumbles which come out of them are simply not to be compared with the class war and personal hatred with which the Conservative cabinet has been alive for the last three years.

One could say that creative tension is mirrored in sterile calm, and certainly the prospect of gradual decline has rather the opposite effect to that of being hanged in a fortnight. The gradual recession of the chance of office has brought out the nicer side of leading Labour men—there is something of a losing-side psychology there, the business of opposition itself has become almost a rosary. Which is all rather sad since, if only the rest of their Party did not exist and if their manifesto could be dropped into oblivion, they would look like a quite attractive alternative Government—cruelly like the Liberals in the late twenties. Except that unlike the Liberals they are not going to be actually destroyed. Labour has an irreducible minority constituency and it is all too likely to be inherited by people who will make Mr Walker, Mr Heseltine and Mr Pym look nice.

3

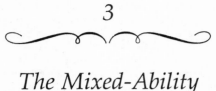

The Mixed-Ability
Comprehensive

The present Conservative cabinet reminds one of a modern sculptor's work in progress, here a lump knocked off with hammer and chisel, additional metal parts welded on with the blowtorch and the artist herself periodically standing back for a view, seeing much improvement but never wholly satisfied.

Mrs Thatcher initially gave herself an Administration which was loaded with continuity, that is with people who regarded her as an aberration and an error of taste. For a long time the disdain for her held by conventional and unchallengeable colleagues continued with a system of cabinet-leaking which would have done credit to a Roman aqueduct. 'A banal suburban little woman' as one of them described her, she was presiding over 'the worst Government for 200 years'. Another Minister used to organize charades based on how best to deride her at his dinner parties. Like the other man quoted he is no longer a Minister. Part of the trouble was social. As one of her young aides put it, 'If I had to sum up her problems in one phrase it would be "the hereditary ruling class".'

It is hardly possible to overestimate the amount of friction existing between men of talent and the sort of *Brideshead* people who put in the handmade boot—to say nothing of that awful English phenomenon, the trainee gentleman. It was one of these, Norman St John-Stevas, who, owing advancement to suburban power, unwisely associated himself with the discontent of the gentry. On him the lady first practised cabinet-making in January 1981. The first reshuffle was a little pilot project which cast poor Stevas into the role of 'the shepherd in Virgil who sought for love and found him a native of the rocks'. It also moved Francis Pym out of Defence, to his

45

vast displeasure, and into the Leadership of the House. The second and major reshuffle came in September 1981 when her nerve was steadier and her eye was in. Sir Ian Gilmour, Lords Soames and Thorneycroft were out. Cecil Parkinson and Norman Tebbit entered the cabinet and *The Times* raged *in Unbekenntnis* at the substitution for people whom it acknowledged socially of those it did not know. But Mrs Thatcher was not only hiring hard talent, she was collecting allies. The third reshuffle was the love-child of the Falklands crisis. Lord Carrington, being encumbered with the consequences of Foreign Office policy, wisely withdrew. Mr Pym, whose seniority offset his growing reputation in the lobbies as 'Availability Pym', went to the Foreign Office where he will feel at home. Mr Biffen, a political friend, though an independent one, was moved from Trade, where he had been less radical than hoped, to the Leadership of the House, a job which disappoints him but one which his horse-melancholy adorns. Lord Cockfield, a portable statistician, was moved from junior Treasury office to Trade, where, startlingly, he gave energetic patronage to those wanting to denationalize anything that didn't move.

It isn't the cabinet of a girl's dreams but it is vastly more in sympathy with what the Prime Minister is trying to do, and its social tone has been agreeably lowered, with Lancaster and Edmonton Grammar Schools replacing Eton and Charterhouse in two Departments. The role of the upper classes, though still around and, like the land-mine, not to be treated casually, has been diminished since Mrs Thatcher's accession to the Tory leadership. Then, an excited Member, observing with pleasure her choice of the stupefyingly uninteresting Adam Butler as PPS, said with innocent delight, 'But that will give her entrée to all the Great Houses.' On occasions like that one feels that the French knew what they were doing in the September Massacres.

The great social bridge between these groups has been Mr Whitelaw. Alone of the gentry element in the cabinet, he liked and respected Mrs Thatcher—not that he is overmuch given to hating or despising generally. He was under violent attack last year as a result of a half-demented Irishman wandering through the ranks of card-playing Palace policemen into the Royal Bedroom. The other half of Mr Whitelaw's trouble came from the suggestion that great tracts of the Metropolitan Police Force were accessories before, after and during the fact of every crime in the calendar, and were being covered up—to avoid scandal.

Nobody would be Home Secretary who could get a job refereeing sumo wrestling. And the police iniquities facing Mr Whitelaw 'are from eternity and shall not fail'. Everyone has known for years that the London police were operating in the great tradition of Jonathan Wild (Thieftaker-General, early advocate of profit-sharing, hanged at Tyburn, 1725). But a succession of Home Secretaries have tried to do good by stealth, hoping that the paper screen of London police reputation would not be ripped up while they worked.

In the Commons Mr Whitelaw, if his pistol misfires, does not knock you down with the butt end; he looks at it quizzically as if to say, 'Now why did that happen?' He is a wonderful (deliberate) sender-up of himself, swaying deftly on the ropes of candid inexpertise. To an agreeable extent he is one of us, not affecting technical one-upmanship— indeed his basic approach is to be strategically one down. A large part of politics has to do with using jargon and figures to create a fallacious impression of whizz-bang accomplishment. To do it unskilfully is to invite precipitation into a tiger pit; to do it well is to begin a parting of the ways from the human race. Not to do it at all is smart.

When standing in at Prime Minister's Questions, Mr Whitelaw has come close to thanking God that he knows nothing about economics. He operates in little rushes, working up bursts of enthusiasm/indignation/earnestness as the situation requires. He is a proper politician, very well aware that government is not a crusade but a camel-ride, with all the bumps, falls and absurdities attendant on such forms of transport. Although naturally compassionate, he has never traded on compassion, and unlike most of the aristocratic element lacks that touch of neurosis which makes the politics of, say, Sir Ian Gilmour so overwrought. Cheerfulness doesn't keep breaking in; it never goes further away than round the corner. It is an old-fashioned style; it might have been expected to fail but it works surprisingly well. He tends to take a statement from about four angles to underline it: '*Do* we have a traffic problem? Of *course* we have a traffic problem. I have never suggested that we do *not* have such a problem. Traffic is one of the most *serious* matters, if I may say so, with which we have to deal. I hope that my view of traffic is *quite* clear.'

As Home Secretary he is actually getting some prisons built, a start on the reclamation of the great area of Departmental neglect over twenty years. 'Great Home Secretaries' are, for the most part, those who ride happily with a fashion, time their off-the-record interviews and their departures well, leaving the boring bricks and mortar to a harassed posterity. Whitelaw, who has become a decidedly unfashionable politician, is mocked by liberals and hated by illiberals, but having got himself the budget he is building at least some of those prisons. The things he will deserve credit for will be those *not* happening, like Attica-style riots. Though the Department has left things perilously late. However he has suffered a melancholy rebuff over immigration regulations, having made changes against which the advocates of tight control and the supporters of wider entry could, and did, cheerfully vote.

But his political importance to this Government is that, while often being in disagreement with its painful policies and holding the seniority and status to have formed a cave against Mrs Thatcher, he refused invitations to do so.

The power of a former Chief Whip with cabinet seniority is enormous; with his neighbour Michael Jopling, he is not unconnected with the making of junior appointments. If Whitelaw had chosen to play factions, then the much treasured scenario of Mrs Thatcher being taken by the arm by a group of senior Ministers and shown out would have been a real option. He was opposed, as a naturally loyal man, to the fevered sectarianism which left some of his colleagues looking like Treshams in search of a Catesby. He is aware of her stubbornness, but he also identifies, along with the courage and strength, a populism in place of the usual élitism. He likes it as something which both works and is fundamentally healthy. The job would not have been his and was not wanted, but he could have played Queen-Breaker. It is not his style. Anyway a sympathy, even an affection, has grown between him and 'that woman'.

One gets some understanding of Whitelaw by looking at Francis Pym and vice versa. On the face of it, give or take a year or two in age, they have affinities. Cumberland Squire and Bedfordshire Squire, successive Chief Whips, old-style politics, not too categorically labelled, men of peace, good chaps both. Anyone who believes that of Pym will buy Vauxhall Bridge. And indeed there must be subscribers for such dream scrip in the Commons where Francis Pym sells as a sincere, disinterested man of the squirearchical country sort, no personal ambition, just anxious to do the best thing. Three years ago it was said that if Mrs Thatcher was run over by a Silver Ghost, 'There wouldn't even be an election. Francis would walk it.' Not quite today. Indeed it is reported that he is feeling unwell and dispirited and no longer expects the leadership. If there is one certain thing in British politics it is that Francis Pym has been running for Downing Street for the best part of a decade. He is a kind of Hattersley under plain cover. He has a pure, elevated and idealistic wish to be Prime Minister. Nothing wrong with that. Mrs Thatcher rose by democratically dropping Mr Heath down a lift shaft and expects life to contain its thrills. But it is an ambition elegantly pomaded and rose-watered with a persuasive and classy patter which leaves the thicker part of the Tory Party seeing dear Francis as the solid gentlemanly type who puts the Party and the country first. When he says, as he often does, 'People are very unhappy', he has a public of one in mind.

Physically he resembles Peter Barkworth playing Baldwin on television. He has vast, grave politeness. He neglects nobody; few actions are not connected with the building-up of goodwill and support. Policies, commitments to any strong beliefs are nowhere discernible. One of his habits is to express interest in the schemes and obsessions of others. It is of course the most effective form of flattery known to man. Tell somebody how much you admire him and he will wonder what you have to do. Tell him that his plan for canal-widening, tariff-imposing or East Anglian devolution is very interesting and you have hooked a ring through his vanity by which he can be taken anywhere. The Pym approach is to say, after a wider meeting, 'My dear fellow, that was a fascinating point you made about the Euro-dollar market. Don't pretend that I understand these specialized economic affairs myself, got my work cut out looking after the estate. But I really would appreciate it if you could spare me half an hour of your very valuable time to explain it to me in greater detail.' In other words, 'Can I come up and see your etchings?' Apply this technique and show an unfailing graciousness, which in a nation with a forelock complex makes those so treated go wobbly about the knees, and one can understand the 'Francis will walk it' scenario.

There is nothing wrong with single-minded ambition for the highest office; the more blood-thirsty city states of the Renaissance would have been lost without it. But, as somebody once unkindly remarked, 'What does he want it *for*?' Perhaps, if we are going to stretch charity a bit, he wants to be a Baldwin, a mild conciliator, a traditional Tory who will go for unity and compromise on all sides— a Tory Harold Wilson. He is helped of course by looking the part— grave, dignified, insubstantial. He is part of the stucco of politics. The one time he showed a flash of quality (and interest in a subject) was at Defence where he wished, not necessarily wrongly, to outspend Treasury limits. But even the most jog-along sort of Tory 'has views' on defence.

Pym is admired by the Stupid Right and deferred to by those who are lost without a gentleman to assure them. He is normality, the normality of the days when it was in order to say 'I don't have any politics, I vote Conservative.' But he would achieve only the crown of a constitutional monarch. The man who would dominate his Government, if Mrs Thatcher does not arrange for him to be privatized, would be the Secretary for Defence Michael Heseltine.

Some people only remember Heseltine picking up the mace in the Commons and swinging it above his head, or making the sort of not very nice mob-orations at Party Conference which the steering committee used to slot into television's intermission period, grateful to have *Trumpton* or *Captain Pugwash* wipe out the impression of worst instincts being brought out in people. By such limited recollection they remember a great deal that is important. Although he now has the Air Marshals he has had really interesting fights at the Environment. And Heseltine's elevation to the running of public buildings and the supervision of local government was a very eloquent appointment. He hated the Environment, believed it beneath him, wanted Industry and, more than any other Minister, yearned for other people's territory. He is indeed able and he is a strenuous worker, keeping late and laborious nights at the office. Much could be explained in terms of frustrated drive and talent compelled for more than three years to be at the mill, if not with slaves, then with the Greater London Council. In practice, the newt-befriending Chairman of the GLC has, by his various defiances, been a good friend to the Minister in terms of headlines generated. They sustained one another like a heraldic Gog and Magog above the municipal plain. Though whether it was wise in so energetic and driving a Minister not to have discouraged a legal campaign against transport subsidy which doubled the travel costs of the commuter is doubtful. But he has this urge to play Beowulf to the Town Hall Grendel. Grendel is still there but there has been lots of publicity. In fairness any Minister of Local Government would have had to fight the councils, many of whom, including Conservative South Oxfordshire, which contains his constituency, are disposed to spend money like Professor Clegg, a drunken sailor and the prodigal son rolled into one. The councils needed a thug and they got one.

The objection to Heseltine is not his capacity but his profoundly dominating personality. Though he performs very competently in the House, it is not a place he likes. Those incidents involving the mace and putting on the Benito at Brighton are not misleading. His style is that of the man saying 'Give me a balcony and I will govern the Home Counties.' He illustrates the illogic of taking the words 'Left' and 'Right' too seriously.

Heseltine has got into Compassion much as others get into gilts or electronics; partly perhaps because being Minister for Merseyside extended his territory a little way, but also because all compassion requires compulsion, spending, plans, organization. It also permitted the Minister to be photographed looking deeply moved in the company of a busload of company directors being shown their duty to the Black and oppressed so recently involved in trying to burn the city down.

That sort of thing is a gimmick, a characteristically bossy gimmick, part of the false politics of 'being seen to do'. It all sounds vaguely progressive and Left of Centre and will satisfyingly involve the spending of some money, though hardly more than token amounts. Yet by contrast those seaside rants in an equally nebulous way gave him a right-wing reputation, not in the economic sense, but as the whipper-up of irrational feelings. And indeed Heseltine, a man who seethes just beneath the surface, tends to take a mobile piazza with him wherever he goes. He speaks against centralization, yet no Minister did more to devolve the Town Halls on to his desk. He is not identifiable with any principle.

It is all rather a pity. Similar energy in a more serene man might have been useful. As Mrs Thatcher presumably well knows, he is not quite her best friend and is sometimes just a little sharp about her. He has been very near to the sharp end of a reshuffle, but like the lesser figure of Peter Walker, he is thought best engaged in Sisyphus-like tasks in a dull Ministry than making trouble on the back benches.

His manner in Parliament is a combination of the perfunctory and the Sir Jasperish. Very little humour, some lofty sarcasm, a catch in the voice which suggests either catarrhal trouble or remote Welsh connections, speaking between a bay and a sneer, but sometimes modulating to a softer tone. He does not drape himself over the dispatch box but addresses it rather like a golf ball, takes a full quota of interventions and handles them proficiently, and these days does not pick up anything more unconstitutional than the folder for his brief. Let us keep it that way. A man on a white horse is best employed as mounted infantry, hence the redeployment to the cost-oblivious military.

His near opposite is John Biffen. There is no perceptible temper in him, not even irritation. From what one hears from his colleagues this has been just as true backstage in his various Departments. But he used to be an embarrassed and nervous speaker, dismissed widely as someone just not up to the rough world of politics.

As it is, he is leading the House, the job which most of all calls for finesse in personal dealings. But it was clear when he started out as Chief Secretary to the Treasury that recovery from a physical illness had disposed of all nerves. Yet he remains gentle. There are two ways of dealing with the Opposition—the fingers round the throat, or the hand on the knee—and Labour has found the chief follower of Enoch Powell enormously seductive. Battling opponents, given to alleging that their grandmothers had been boiled down for glue by the mill owners, would come and take birdseed from his hand. One has seen the large and menacing Eric Heffer make a galumphing interruption, have something—inaudible to the gallery—whispered to him by the Minister, and collapse into happy giggles.

The accent, so rarely for a Tory, is not what is called correct, whether natural or bottle, but Somerset: 'Ai am not surre ai haad quoite that palacy in meind.' Even in jobs which involved the big speeches he was short on peroration, being a conversational, reasoning man. Although all his economic beliefs are Dry, none of the difficulties facing the Government will surprise him. He has never been an evangelist, just a believer in painful necessity. As resident pessimist, his thoughts 'were of trouble and trouble came'.

He probably also overrates the power of things as they are, the ability of civil servants to dig a ha-ha in the route of the most hopeful development. He is just not nasty enough. Yet there must be an element of sadness. Although some of us said, a year in advance, that he would make the ideal Leader of the House for positive reasons, not being an economic Minister probably hurts. Yet if one had to allot a role for this Somerset-born and Shropshire-based man, it is that he will, in an intellectually acute fashion, be the voice of the shires. A Social Democrat Member saw him as a very different kind of voice, but like them, a built-in stabilizer, 'the hard man in a non-Thatcher Government'. He will be the opposite, a mild man under Thatcherism. Not surprisingly, along with Sir Keith Joseph and Nigel Lawson, he voted against the death penalty last year.

He is the ace in any television campaign. So many Conservatives, starting with their leader, upbraid the audience. Heseltine seems close to telling us to stand by our beds; Whitelaw splutters; Pym has great charm for the dimly respectful and a splendid sincerity-substitute; Sir John Nott sounds like a Tannoy test. From the entire cabinet, Biffen stands out as the man who has full human status, who reasons and thus avoids the sort of adman's Hail Mary, whose discourse leaves behind a sense of some nourishment. In an election he should broadcast early and broadcast often.

With Leon Brittan one will be brisk. He is everywhere advertised to us as the cleverest thing since cybernetics, a bright light shining in Cleveland and Whitby, a computer, known to the Office as 'Leon'. But in Parliament and, if possible, even more so on television, he is an ambulating catastrophe. He doesn't lose his place, doesn't read a script in an inaudible monotone like his boss, Sir Geoffrey, who has done for tedium what Ray Reardon did for snooker. Unlike Jim Prior he does not get huffily hot and indignant. There are lots of speaking faults he does *not* have. He doesn't need them. Put it this way, the Government is engaged in a policy which was bound to hurt in the short run even if world markets had been easy and which, since world markets are hard, hurts long and achingly. With reason it can argue that it is handling the consequences of thirty years of uneconomic wages and uneconomic money even if it has made some mistakes of its own. But the need to make the case well, in quiet detail, is enormous. There is actually quite a good case . . . as long as Brittan doesn't make it.

He does not mean to sound arrogant and patronizing, or to give the impression that only a fool could have asked the last question. It is not a matter of Brittan being arrogant and patronizing in himself; he can be very likeable, but in public he is on the losing end of a Cambridge manner. He seems at times to be talking through molasses. There is nothing unpleasant there, simply a want of felicity, of sympathetic ordinariness—the consequence perhaps of having great gifts and not mingling overmuch with fallible humanity. As a barrister, Mr Brittan did of course have to defend rapists and muggers; and he is happiest in academic company; but for those between rapists and wranglers, a broad grouping which includes most MPs, Mr Brittan seems to have little touch.

Mrs Thatcher has been deft at handling the people most likely to give her trouble. Mr Peter Walker has been set one of the labours of Hercules without the least prospect of achieving it. As Minister of Agriculture he was obliged to negotiate the Common Fisheries Agreement with our 'Community partners'. Since his friend and patron, Mr Heath, signed a document ten years ago which said that unless we agreed to a voluntary share-out of our fishing rights and coastal waters our partners would have the automatic right on 1 January 1983 to fish up to our beaches, even Mr Walker, partner with Mr Slater in a hundred and one things a boy can do with a secondary bank, was helpless. He protested his superb efforts in the correspondence-course accent which is the mark of an older school of self-made Conservatives, but it is all futile. He had been dealt a hand of deuces and threes—Grimsby, Hull and the other fishing ports have sold their boats and virtually acknowledged death. Industry has grave problems, but if it was in the trouble which Mr Heath put fishing into, ICI would be selling its goods off a tray. Despite the distinguished marcelled hair, the affectation of hauteur at the dispatch box, Walker, former passionate opponent of Europe, at a politic hour turned passionate European, swings slowly, with faint clanking noises, on a gibbet of his own devising.

James Prior, who must be dissuaded from a demotic/Anglican urge to be called 'Jim', something which makes him sound like a suffragan bishop, performs rather well in the House. He is of course what in Lancashire used to be called a 'worrit'. A pink and grey man of modest stature, he always seems to be rushing, even when going 'step by step'—like a tortoise with an outboard motor. As a debater he is not tested by the other side except for their maddening habit of congratulating him. It is not good for a politician to be the Opposition's definition of the one statesman on the Government benches. But this is made up for by the determination of large sections of the Conservative Party to throw things at him. After Employment, where he developed immobilism into the higher form of marginalism, he lurched at Northern Ireland into the sort of activity which his previous Department might have devised to keep the unemployment figures down.

The Northern Ireland Assemblies Bill provides for the sort of non-legislating, non-revising, non-constituent and only fractionally consultative Assembly, whose self-evident idleness will assuredly elect Satan into the Speaker's chair. It is, by a degree, actually less useful than the European Assembly, something previously thought incapable of accomplishment. It scares the Protestants into expectations of its being stage one for a link-up and, later, a merger with the Dublin Dáil, while doing no such thing for the Catholics, who refuse to sit. As a consequence the only Ulster politician to contemplate the Assembly with any sort of pleasure is Mr Ian Paisley. This Bill Mr Prior earnestly and ardently put through, finally obtaining a guillotine after the House had deliberated until it dropped.

It might though be a mistake to overestimate the animus between him and Mrs Thatcher. He is her opponent on a number of issues but he has always been a candid opponent, actually standing up to her, winning the title of 'No, Margaret', hardly the mark of a negligible or surreptitious man. He is not feverishly ambitious, he is not spiteful, nor, despite his duke's-steward-type role as a former estate manager, is he truly part of the coronet Camorra. He was legitimately loyal to Mr Heath who had superintended his career, though there are signs of exhausted patience with that clanking and over-exposed apparition.

The serious criticism to be made of Mr Prior is that he has had a defensive and defeatist view of the Left in politics—both of the unions and of the Labour Party. He is at one with those for whom Conservative government is a matter of minimizing retreat from a militancy which has history on its side. Those who are most apprehensive of Marxism frequently practise an inverted Marxism of their own. If you believe that you are playing for time against eternity on the big issues it is not uncommon to have a passion for simulation and tinkering on the little ones. The Northern Ireland Bill is part of a political baroque—not exuberance but the desperate construction of administrative swags and cherubs to fill in time before the End.

He has one other problem. I said he was not excessively ambitious, but said nothing of his wife. Jane Prior is, of all cabinet wives, the one most dedicated to her husband's destiny, so much so that she has been known, when dissatisfied with his answers to interviewers' questions, to prorogue him and substitute her own. One encounter for a feature article in a popular newspaper ran like this:

Questioner: Tell me, Mr Prior, what do you think about the problems of X?

Mr Prior: Well, I think that X is a very tricky business and that. . . .

Mrs Prior: What Jim means is that we shall have to take decisive action on X and he has firm plans to do so.

Mr Prior: Yes, my dear.

Any man caught, in this male-persecuting age, betwixt Jane Prior at home and Margaret Thatcher at work, deserves our warm feelings; if the experience has driven him to legislation rather than drink, we should be understanding. He is a decent man, a worrier, a brave critic but someone who functions in the open.

Poor Sir John Nott. What else can one say? He is an extremely intelligent, quick-minded man and was one of the few adornments to the Tory front bench when it came to debate. But the cleverest men encounter difficulties when rounding off the corners of a square. Sir John, to his lasting credit, was as direct as one should expect a politician to be. (And, frankly, one is not briefed to be Minister of Defence against Argentina.) Saving Sir John became an impossible exercise. He had two sets of political enemies. There is the Old Right, who tend to want defence spending, and in particular naval spending, rather as Mr Reagan wanted them, not comprehending the connection between this and high interest rates. So from being poised for the Exchequer, a job he is fit and suited for, he is returning to Cornwall and to discreet retirement with hazards. The lean didactic presence—all elbows and bone structure, often funny, usually instructive and laced with curry, will disappear. That is a loss of talent, a rectilinear elegance, a gloomy and amusing man who told the truth as he saw it only to bring out against him the Lieutenant Commanders (Rtd) and a sharp, unexpected S-bend of history called the Falklands war.

The Secretary of State for Industry was once cruelly observed in his days as Health Secretary with the feminine remark 'Yes, I know, but who else is there?' Yet she let him go on and up and he now dreams of the Exchequer for which, as a previous Treasury Junior Minister, he has the form. But, so far as the chamber is concerned, he never quite connects, never wholly fails. Patrick Jenkin, blue-black haired, tall, heavy spectacled, is a sketch writer's nightmare. He doesn't dazzle nor does he fall on his face, apart from a single episode when Jeff Rooker came down from the hills like a statistical Afghan tribesman. He is mildly boring but not in the sort of fire-engine-stopping, special-entry-for-the-Venice-Biennale way in which Sir Geoffrey is boring. Jenkin is simply the solid, competent Minister who knows his figures, who is courteous but not Castilian, and who makes the odd little joke which without being a disaster would have been better not made. The chief interest is to see him struggle with his shadow—on the Health half of his job—the unspeakable Mrs Dunwoody, a lady whose tirading doorstep bombast would make any damsel-devouring dragon take the nearest bypass. Jenkin, a man of genuine Christian devotion, must regard Mrs Dunwoody as a tribulation sent to test him.

His Christianity is important. Jenkin is a believer and one who impresses the unbelieving onlooker. Anyone in trouble is his concern. Any of his colleagues whose luck turns is likely to find his efforts over their constituency matters increased, any person needing help is helped.

There are similarities, not often picked up, with Sir Keith Joseph whose unhappiness seems to give so many unengaging people so much pleasure. Joseph is the butt of much unkindness and ignorance, starting with the sub-adolescents of *Private Eye*. But those who work with him do not talk like that. Norman Tebbit, his deputy at Industry until September 1981, speaks of 'the kindest, gentlest, most considerate person I have met', and there are many echoes of this among those working with Joseph. In the House he is supposed to be a poor speaker but only if you expect flash simplicities. He has an elaborating, cogitating sort of mind which takes up parenthetical issues which detract from the main business. His great fault used to be a willingness to accept endless interruptions and try to deal with them seriously. This was not good for the timetable of the train of thought. But he gives way much less now and speaks rather well in debate. But to get the value of Joseph you have to accept that he is a don with a very strong conscience rather than a routine politician.

Having joined in general reflationary policy in 1972–3 he promoted the NHS reorganization. This, he openly says, was wrong. The remark was everywhere received by the trade in terms of a Bateman cartoon—'The man who said his policy had been mistaken!' Think of the errors which have *not* been admitted—the Humber Bridge, Concorde (step forward about twenty-seven Ministers of both Parties), VAT increases, the Clegg Report, the Common Agriculture Policy, panda cars, the Scarman Report, *détente*, Buzby? And while they all took place, nobody actually committed them—or if they did, it wasn't murder but manslaughter. But when a politician says 'I was wrong' he is everywhere accused of agonizing.

Joseph in his mild way is, of course, the man who had the temerity to get the Conservative Party to think. He can hardly expect to be forgiven.

If I do not linger over the Chancellor it will be because he has been dragged, murmuring and querying, into the narrative several times already. The ability of Sir Geoffrey to turn *King Lear* into a Chancery suit is not doubted. What astounds is the perpetual mildness of the man. He does not rage, he barely essays a snap and hardly ever comes within the outer suburbs of peevishness. In the plump Chancellor there is just a hint of Pigling Bland. He is another male victim, though Lady Howe is not in Jane Prior's league and was long kept engaged by that Alp of inutility, the Equal Opportunities Commission.

Perhaps Sir Geoffrey gets his satisfaction from watching the reflaters turn from rose to scarlet to porphyry. His great talent is for telling hungry sheep about the cost of grass. He regards policy as a matter of reason, to be defended rationally. This may account for his lack of rapport with the Commons and also for his often effective one-to-one television discussions. Pitched in the House against Peter Shore, his Welsh phlegm is lit by the incendiary attacks of his opponent's English fire and eloquence. But Howe is another of these barristers in politics, a very wearing commodity. The brief becomes holy writ, there are no excursions, not much alacrity at handling unforeseen questions, none of the little acts of deftness by which some politicians keep the *causerie* interesting, and little partisan feeling. Of course Sir Geoffrey has courage, is honest, has a discernible likeability beneath the Middle Temple basalt, but listening to him is not an indoor recreation.

David Howell at Transport has for some time been everybody's hot tip for the water chute. He was compelled to lose on wage settlements and on the failure to close down a small group of pits as economic as wooden ploughs. Highly intelligent, he is more than something of a ditherer and inclined to clap himself into the chainmail of 'the Minister speaking officially said. . . .' Mrs Thatcher's attitude was based on the old Baldwin theory that he would not pick a fight with the Pope, the Farmers or the Mineworkers. In the manner of generals fighting the last war she almost certainly overestimated the power of Arthur Scargill to bite the throat out of the economy, and signalled general retreat on that front. Poor David Howell was left to make a Ministerial statement on the continuity and consistency of Government policy and its willingness to look anew at wooden ploughs as aids to production.

At Transport he was correspondingly fortunate to be present when the Prime Minister decided that Mr Buckton was unpopular enough and small enough to be worth fighting. Howell therefore presided over the expulsion of the school bully, something which went down like sherbet among mixed infants, but only because Mrs Thatcher proposed and the TUC disposed.

Howell is nowhere disliked, nowhere feared. At the dispatch box he has enough nervous tension to run a small generator and while assured Ministers either fold themselves lazily over the box to begin discourse or lean back as if contemplating the fairway, Howell frequently clutches both sides of it in the hope that it will not explode. He is one of the nice men but the victim of his own uncertainty, not least because he came up through the Conservative Party's private civil service. He is accordingly geared for subordination, something which could prolong his career providing that at all times he arranges to be Kosygin to somebody else's Brezhnev.

The contrast with Nigel Lawson at Energy could not be more absolute. Lawson has all the humility of a heavy dragoon. Like Brittan he sounds arrogant. Unlike Brittan he means it. He has not the remotest interest in 'assuring the Honourable Gentleman opposite' of anything, even if that formula escapes his lips. The lip curls, voluntarily. If Mrs Thatcher ever reassesses the standing of the miners, Arthur versus Nigel will be something to watch— spurio-toiler against the unapologetic face of the City. Lawson is on nobody's shortlist of future Prime Ministers because he has never bothered to please. But the arrogance is more agreeable than Heseltine's. It derives from a belief that markets, banks, the whole apparatus of capitalism are good things and not to be excused nervously or given PR treatment as deserving a small measure of tolerance.

Few people have quite got the hang of Norman Fowler at Health and Social Security. He is not a gentleman, which is a good start; and despite service on *The Times* speaks with an accent which ten years ago would have barred him from any but token presence on the Tory benches. His advancement is not popular. He is seen as pushy; he *is* pushy. At a time when the Government seemed to have become a painted ship of inanition, Fowler ended restrictions on coach transport, stood on British Rail's instep and made himself.

As a speaker he is a human tablecloth; lank hair and large black-framed glasses dominate a slight physique while he does a digital job explaining things to the Opposition. Not rude like Lawson, though not exactly a man with a taste for phrase and language, he manages to make front-bench speeches sound a little like rather punchy adult education. How far he will really go, whether Transport was a single shrewd stroke and whether the DHSS—with its waiting chorus of outraged nurses doing their *Trojan Women* bit, and NUPE members (the Guild of Waste)—will not overwhelm him, is the question. The DHSS has, after all, a larger budget—£13 billion—than many small countries. Conceivably one of the less tolerant Khans might have brought it under control, but Norman in all his glory will surely finish up treading the same hamster's wheel, holding down wages—for a bit—only to see the numbers employed going up. One of our problems is that we have the wrong unemployment. Mills and drop forges go under, hospital administrators and kitchen porters have the lifespan of Struldbruggs. Mr Fowler is a good Minister but not good enough to create order here: God possibly...?

Let us leave out Cecil Parkinson who is the fourth or fifth most important man in the cabinet but who is present in the Commons under the same Carthusian vows (well, silence anyway, and obedience if he has any sense) as the Chief Whip. So he is only hazily remembered in the House from long ago in 1981 as number two at Trade, on flying visits between selling electric circuits to Equador.

But look at his friend Norman Tebbit. If politicians were stocks on a futures market, the present writer could have withdrawn to a

Tuscan villa on the proceeds of going deep on Tebbits when they were a penny stock. The Secretary for Employment has been the Racal of politics. Dismissed universally in the seventies as a boorish, back-bench bicycle-chain specialist given to a savage direct combativeness, he has become a blue chip and by no means overpriced. The ascent has been outstanding.

His early hard-man stuff endeared him to Mrs Thatcher, whose supporter he has been from the start. The Tories had proved emotionally unable to cope with the Opposition during 1970–4. They know how to be arrogant, to snub, cut or crush individuals socially. But faced with noise and abuse they crumbled into abjection, either reading the brief or begging to be heard and assuring public and opponents that they were deeply moderate and that their position was nearer to that of the Opposition than anyone supposed. Tebbit, who arrived in 1970, not only shouted back; if anything was thrown he threw it back. He was a one-man Israeli Air Force, who, instead of ineffectual spluttering or limp meekness, could return ill for ill on a satisfyingly Old Testament basis. When Mrs Thatcher became leader he kept up the bad work, but was also drawn into a small group of the like-minded who briefed her on hard questions to ask and unpleasant things to say. But his reputation in May 1979 was still that of Vlad the Chauffeur, a hired assassin, perhaps also useful as a bodyguard.

Yet it had been apparent for anyone with ears that the back-bench brass-knuckle stuff was also clever and funny and that only a very able man could have upset Labour as well as he did. Tebbit is a professional cracksman who, having broken into office, is not only staying there but showing signs of working up to the thirty-second floor. He has the gift of adjustment. Hooliganism as a profession was seen in the light of Sammy Glick's remark on his first job: 'Yeah, it's a good job now. It won't be a good one next year.'

Tebbit was fairly bored by 1979 with the role of 'Shall I do him over boss?' and rose to speak for the first time as Parliamentary Under-Secretary for Trade with the untroubled facility of one who had never intended doing anything else. He horrified Labour by a combination of civility and Ministerial grasp which struck some of them as unfair. And many opponents are still fighting him as if he was irregular cavalry taking no casualties, uncomprehending of the quite different tactics of a gazetted general who is cunningly using textbook tactics in Maquis country.

Two years were spent denouncing Tebbit for the dreadful, uncouth fellow that he was, to which the Minister (quickly advanced to number two at Industry) turned a mild, slightly hurt response at such regrettable personal tactics. The Departmental embrace has not extinguished his asperity and love of the sardonic. A group of trade unionists once visiting with a view to hectoring him were cut off at the first sentence with 'This is one of my less sympathetic mornings. I have this urge to nail somebody to the wall opposite and see no reason, gentlemen, why that somebody shouldn't be you. Now what can I do for you?' But this is half the trick of it. Everyone knows that the assassin has not hung up his daggers, merely that he uses them more sparingly. Debates are therefore conducted in the fear of what he *might* do. He can thus afford to be positively gentle while not forgetting to be funny or interesting. Savage attacks establish a reputation, but often used they win diminishing returns. He is a natural debater, one of those rare people who bring MPs and journalists back into the chamber and gallery. His command is so total that he has made it a set practice to give way to all interventions with the words 'Of course' in the certain knowledge that not he but the intervenor puts his head at risk.

He is also part of the social change in Tory politics. Mr Harold Macmillan, holding court at Pratt's Club among cronies, observed recently 'Was listenin' to extracts from a debate in the House on the wireless—some cockney feller speakin'. They tell me he is one of Her Majesty's Ministers.' Another rather less well-known politician was complaining in print about 'the petit-embourgeoisement of our Party'. The lower middle classes are showing signs of getting above themselves ... and doing so on their own terms. Tebbit does indeed speak with an accent, more precisely an outer North London one and, since he speaks more effectively than his betters, he sees no occasion to amend it. 'I am not a gentleman,' he has said more than once with some passion. Talent has usually been able to battle its way up but Tebbit's sort of man does not feel any need to disown his roots or manicure his vowels. Coming as he does from the social group most unacceptable to sociologists, the one encompassing lower middle and upper working classes, having been something useful and difficult (a long distance BOAC pilot), he has neither the guilty feelings of the Social Democratic Duke of Devonshire, nor Heseltine's instinct to play compassion as a card. His recurring theme is common sense.

In addition to his Trade Union Act, his Green Paper indicates that he will be preparing a Union election ballot Bill, ideally for discussion now and enaction in the event of re-election which its prospect would make more likely.

The only worry about Norman Tebbit is paradoxically whether he is hard enough. The best debater the Tories have had since Iain Macleod, everywhere praised for his grasp of facts and evidence, shrewd enough to know all about 'the hobgoblin of little minds', he is not in any deep sense ruthless. There is a streak of amiability and of caution. And, partly as a result of circumstances, he has finished up as a big spender—at Industry where under Sir Keith he handled the British Steel business and BL. Any narrow consistency would certainly have drawn the line at the BL investment, and it would have had grave doubts about the training scheme. But the amiability, little supposed among casual commentators, has made him extremely popular within his own Party. Typically he enjoys Parliament, unlike Heseltine who pays it state visits. He is going up for sure. Either the Home Office, to which his deputy, David Waddington, has gone ahead as Minister of State, or the Exchequer could come his way as the present occupants ultimately and honourably depart. He is six years the junior of Mrs Thatcher; she advanced him and he is undeviatingly of her personal party. If the Tories were to hit a long winning streak and she left in her own time of her own volition (major assumptions), there might be 'some cockney feller speakin'. They tell me he's Her Majesty's First Minister.'

4

The Nothingburger

'Ah yes,' said a Serbian friend of mine, who lives in this country, 'the SDP. I always think of them as a Czech party.' Urban, middle class, intelligent, reasonable, short on peasants, long on people with second degrees if not quite yet afflicted with that melancholy which is a mark of the Czech people, they go a long way to fitting the observation.

As a force in the House of Commons the SDP amounts to very little more than not very much. With the single exception of Dr Owen who seems to have wandered in from the leading role in a boulevard play, all profile and brass neck, they do not leave any sort of stamp on the Commons. They are as much afflicted by their own hierarchy as by the Curia of an anti-Pope. The Gang of Four, as they tirelessly and tiresomely describe themselves, must be getting something like 85 per cent of the party's exposure. This is not entirely due to egotistical vanity, though a good deal is just that.

Rodgers, Williams, Owen and Jenkins (come to think of it they sound like a Welsh Party) took a big risk leaving their Labour Party status of para-cabinet rank. However affable, they cling tightly to the enhanced billing in a smaller, perhaps disappearing, theatre. In fairness they can argue that the world in its ignorance had heard only of the big names and to concentrate public attention they should hog the lights. Humankind cannot perhaps bear too much Social Democracy.

Even more than the Tories they owe a debt to modern techniques of publicity and promotion, a species of non-carnal pimping. The launch was held in a way both chic and well timed for the evening papers: at breakfast—at the Connaught Rooms. The red-white-and-

blue logo 'SDP' was everywhere. The Four sat on a raised dais, the
eleven defecting members (more were to follow) sat on a lowered
dais. Questions were put by the press. The Four spoke, the eleven
kept dutifully silent. Plastic folders containing publicity material
were distributed. We were told that the mould should be broken,
and that people were tired of old adversarial politics, and, quite
reasonably, that detailed SDP policies would have to wait for
development. On the strength of proposals made since—twelve
Regional Prime Ministers and all—absence of policy was the least of
their problems. The biggest mistake they have made has been to
play at manifestos. It shows a misunderstanding of their main
strength, which was a high tide of negation; for a while they were
popular for what they were not. Give or take the odd Tammany
Irish member, they are a respectable Party, though Mr Jenkins's
'remuneration' from the Vision and the Ideal, at £60,000 a year (not
quite double the earnings of a Fleet Street Linotyper) plus the sort of
severance money you could roll over in may prove embarrassing.
Yet they are a clean Party. Their MPs are frequently oppressively
clones of the quiet-and-well-behaved-young-man-hoping-to-be-
made-a-Junior-Minister sort. Roper, Wrigglesworth, Cartwright,
Bradley, all are washed, properly dressed, tending to wear suits,
well spoken, sons any mother would be proud to have, and with
about a quarter of an ounce of personality between them.

Yet this is no defect with the public. It dislikes the Assyrian
quality of those now taking over the Labour Party; it intermittently
finds Mrs Thatcher and Sir Geoffrey a great strain. It would love a
soft option. The SDP, linked with the Liberals, should represent a
soft option with oomph, the zero option of politics. It should be
mocked all right but also taken seriously. There has been a general
decline in the take of the two great parties combined over a
succession of general elections. The bland insubstance of the SDP
and the Liberals is blotting paper made to collect such spillings.
Over decades the rise of the Swedish Centre Party from a small
special-interest group called the Farmers' Party until it was large
enough to form the core of a coalition which replaced, ironically,
the Swedish Social Democratic Party, is instructive. But Mr
Gunnar Hedlund, who brought off this slow-motion coup,
had the advantage of proportional representation. And the British
SDP *cares passionately* for PR; indeed it adores both meanings of the
term 'PR'.

Not only does the SDP have one continental model in mind, their
very name, Social Democratic Party, and its initials are a coy,
esteeming echo of the German Sozial-Demokratische Partei
Deutschlands—SPD. They are good internationalists but also they
are a Party in pursuit of somebody else's identity, an empty looking-
glass seeking to be quarter-lit by what borrowings and reflections it

can. None of this is political criticism. Precisely because the SDP is a conspiracy of inadequacy it may be perfectly designed for a disgruntled, amiable, soft-line electorate. For certain it is working as a magnet for discontented Conservatives vastly more than Labour voters. The chances of Mr Rodgers being re-elected in Stockton or of the very bright Mr Horam holding on to Gateshead West are non-existent. They can lose or they can fight southern suburban seats, or possibly both. The one constant in the next election is that Labour, even with Mr Foot's actual and perceived faults, with the polytechnic lecturers at the gate, has an irreducible laager of around 220 seats and a sort of sullen immortality.

One might have supposed that the Social Democrats, the creation of the defects of the Labour Party, ought to be challenging Labour and taking Labour seats. After all, the Labour voter does not think as Ken Livingstone thinks. But Labour is a working-class party if it is anything at all, and the SDP does not sound, does not look, cannot be, working class. Of course it means well by all those Slovak peasants; every civility is expressed but they cannot get across to one another.

There are several reasons for this, not least the outflanking of the Social Democrats by working-class voters taking positions more 'right-wing' than them on issues like law and order; and like the Falklands where, apart from the Doctor, the SDP spent most of the time with its head under the eiderdown. A thoroughly aggressive and articulated support for that expedition would have been good politics; it would even have shown an understanding of the British people and of their bloody-minded patriotism. King George V with his 'I hate abroad' could have given the SDP sound advice. Not that it is in their nature to take advice. They know. For this limp-handed internationalism and dislike of vulgar truculence is engraved on the signet ring of Roy Jenkins, and the main grouping in the Party derives from the circle known in the sixties and seventies as the 'Friends of Roy Jenkins'. They start with certainties—an unreserved commitment to the EEC and a belief in being 'civilized' (whatever that is!). They are liberal-progressive without reservation, very Rousseau-like in their urge to get the chains off and let every monster lurch jovially towards the Bethlehem of his choice. Facile liberalism still rules and loses working-class votes. The SDP has not yet been mugged, but wait until the next general election. Accordingly it has the illusions to sustain the good will of great regiments of influential people—civil servants, the command structures of *The Times, Observer* and *Guardian* who can indeed pump the balloon, but who have on their own account enough votes to seize control of only a modest parish council.

Indeed the make-up and the outside support of the SDP was determined long before the break with Labour. And the new party carries the narcissistic weaknesses of the private grouping which at its tightest and narrowest definition was Jenkins, Dick Taverne, David Marquand and John Harris, though much expanded in Parliament by the efforts of Bill Rodgers. Good on the economy, sensible, though never quite as forceful as they needed to be on the grave and nasty nature of the Far Left, uncritically Bruxellois on the EEC, sodden wet on crime and punishment, lacking instinct and affection for people who work with their hands, and afflicted with a snobbery of style and company, they even have a touch of Louis XIV's court. It is not, perhaps, quite enough.

There is a sense in which a slightly phoney, but good-natured, orthodox Labour politician like Neil Kinnock does have a liking for industrial workers and can convey feelings which the remote and rather didactic SDP politicians cannot approach. They have all the virtues of an elect except fanaticism; as my Serbian friend put it about the Czechs, they are over-civilized. None of this unkindness means that they have to fail. The high gloss which preceded the Falklands will not come back, but the negative attraction is still there—especially for the Stupid Left of the Tory Party. Their plan of campaign just has to be different. It must revert to one of marching not through Georgia, but Wiltshire. There are pickings to be taken, not from the workers or those out of work, but from guilty, Danegeld-paying, soft Conservatives who want to be nice, want to be enlightened and who live in places secure from the consequences of enlightenment; people who flinch from whatever virtues the Thatcher Government may have.

There was quite a little buzz in the latter part of 1981 that the SDP would succeed in drawing four or five Conservative MPs across the floor. Names which were mentioned mistakenly included Mr Robert Hicks, who has anxieties at the strength of the Liberals in his West Country seat, and Mr Hugh Dykes, sick at heart at the non-occurrence of promotion. There were others, but the Social Democrats had to make do with Mr Christopher Brocklebank-Fowler, a dim and dandyish half-pennyworth of profile who made a shrill little speech in the House about the evils of blue corners and red corners and then strode down the aisle and across the floor to the handshakes and applause of Social Democrats . . . and who has not been heard from since. It was an Alpine yodel but it didn't start an avalanche.

But 'Marching through Wiltshire' remains the only ploy open to the SDP and their Liberal allies. The sort of seats which could be vulnerable are those in which the aggregate and average income of the population should be as safe for the Tories as Stonehenge for the Druids, but which a really idle, futile MP of the kind better not named have undermined by their want of trouble. Or there are the constituencies which perfectly conscientious Members like Mr

Hicks at Bodmin or Mr Charles Morrison at Devizes have found too safe for comfort.

Their electorates, seeing no left-wing bugaboo west of Hammersmith, feel themselves at liberty to flirt with the Liberals. They are always less vulnerable at general elections despite the best efforts of Labour voters who frequently leave their candidate without a deposit in their earnest rush to stick a finger in the Conservative eye. The sharper Tories have noticed that such losses could be generously repaid in more marginal seats if SDP or Liberal candidates without hope of winning were to siphon off a number of otherwise Tory votes sufficient to elect a Labour candidate on a minority vote. The prospect of making a back for the next Labour Government was not what the SDP was meant to be about at all.

What the new Party must realistically hope for is to pick up enough seats from the Tories (while helping Labour a little but not too much) so as to be able to play arbitrator in a Parliament so hung that it contains no majority Party. From this would flow an alliance, either with the Tories or with Labour; proportional representation would be enacted by statute, the SDP and Liberal alliance would then be guaranteed about 120 seats at any election, permanent coalition party status, red boxes and Daimler Sovereigns with official drivers. It is called a programme of radical reform.

The fact that it involves putting reinforced concrete round the real status quo—giving us the wisdom of the last twenty years: incomes policies, boards of wise men, local government reorganization, consultations involving the TUC and CBI, payment of all demands made by the French to support the production of food incapable of sale and not destined for consumption, and, at a guess, the building of a second Humber Bridge—is not for us to decry. We are only the electorate; and the beauty of PR is that it liberates politicians. They become free to engage in *combinazione*. Civil servants, whatever their powers now, would find life inside such a sand-castle a glory beyond their dreams. No consensual, space-occupying alliance is going to do anything radical.

Indeed there may be votes in it for them to say so. M. Mitterrand's advisers coined a sweet phrase worth a special bonus on Madison Avenue—'la force tranquille'. Anyone with the wit to offer people tranquillity, business as usual, stability and dullness has got smart and is fifteen under par at the last hole.

However (and there is quite an elephant pit of 'howevers' for the SDP), by 'stability' people, very reasonably, mean nothing at all—a Government with all the ceremonial presence and functional inutility of the Monarchy. And the SDP (and the Liberals for that matter) are perfervid doers. By 'stability' they mean, for example, the reopening of devolution just after the lid of that can had been jammed on; they mean regional Parliaments; they mean reform of the House of Lords. In short they will be the most ardent meddlers, devoted treaders of the hamster's wheel. Also with so many things going for them, they do not have the wisdom of silence, that Coolidge touch which wins elections.

All that was necessary was to say 'We are not Mrs Thatcher, who is a hard-faced woman, nor are we the Labour Party, which wants to nationalize front gardens and is increasingly dominated by young men with the qualities of the nicer members of the *Sturm-Abteilung*—and we will leave you alone.' It is hard to see how they could have been stopped. Moderation is a verbal hand-grenade in English conversations. But even without their inability to resist the formation of policy study groups, and the thunderbolt of the Falklands, I suspect they would still have slowed down.

And some of the reason for this is apparent in Parliament. The SDP has plenty of talent. For a small party of thirty members it has a disproportionate amount, but it isn't parliamentary talent. They have never begun to make an impression on the House. Enoch Powell carries more authority than all thirty of them rolled together ... and carries it even with the people who detest him. The best the new Party has to offer is the mellowed arrogance of Dr Owen.

The SDP was beautifully thought out. It moved forward in the early days just enough to keep itself in the headlines, not so fast as to lose its reserves of new events to announce. The other parties were kept in nervous, cursing apprehension of the next opinion poll. They broke 50 per cent of the electorate and were showing up, however unrealistically, on the psephologists' charts with columns of between 450 and 520 seats. The achievement—even if it now disintegrates into ashes and rose-water—will still have been astonishing. Difficult as its own act became to follow, and awful its luck with the Falklands, there was still no need for collapse.

The rate of deceleration would depend on the members of the new Party. And failure here has started with the systematic inability of Mr Jenkins, for all the glory which played around his head for some of the more impressionable columnists, to sound like a force for anything. He indicated at Warrington, where he narrowly lost to an unpleasing person called Douglas Hoyle in a Labour citadel seat, just how very good he had been. It was an old-fashioned election and better for it, strong on proper meetings with large audiences and reasoned expositions. He played up-market but he played it humorously, visibly and was self-evidently picking up votes whenever he held a meeting.

At Glasgow Hillhead he was less impressive, still speaking seriously to well-attended meetings, but easily despondent, sending out waves of depression from his camp, showing signs of irritation at having so hard a fight after Mrs Williams's triumph in Crosby. (Private jealousies have hung around a Party far too narrowly based, not to say in the profession of being nice, to be able to afford them.) He was not entirely well which explained something, but there was such a contrast with the zest with which he had run at Warrington. Even so, nothing, even in his Glasgow performance, explains his total failure to so much as light a lucifer in the Commons since election.

His presence as a Scottish member is not the natural thing it was when Asquith, Birrell and Haldane sat on a hill somewhere in Fifeshire and looked down on three constituencies 'each gratefully represented by a London barrister'. (I misquote from memory *Asquith*, the biography written by Mr Roy Jenkins.) Hillhead is a slightly absurd seat for him to be representing, and not a safe one with redistribution taking place. Not even to disoblige the Conservatives do Scottish Labour voters amend their habits.

And performed he hasn't. The mannerisms which were a cheeky adornment at the height of his career are now getting their own back. All the affectations of manner, the fluttering hands, the lisp, the 'I feel bound to say', which some of his close followers actually reproduce in conversation, seem to have acquired a controlling interest in the man. As for that accent, if Jenkins were not so rich he could get a disability pension for it. He is ill equipped for the rougher side of life in the Commons, not least because he has enjoyed an excess of civil discourse in Brussels, give or take the odd obstreperous French Agriculture Minister. (Brussels rows are more sulks than bawling matches anyway.) The House of Commons is something of a problem comprehensive, and an ability to handle the underprivileged and potentially violent members of society is a prerequisite in any master. The headmistress keeps order like a prison visitor of the less sympathetic sort; Mr Powell, the classics master, does it by sheer fascination, but some masters never quite keep the class in awe and the ink pellets fly.

Mr Jenkins has made only one successful speech since his return from the wilderness and that was by way of an exercise in light entertainment. During the Falklands Enquiry Debate, the amateur historian in Jenkins got off the leash, stopped being responsible and romped all over the common fetching sticks and pairs of trousers from every episode since the Crimean War. It was a pleasant piece of mischief decked out with an apparatus of learning but, even as a lark, a distinct cut above the House of Commons norm. The people who have been heckling and persecuting Jenkins fell silent. If he is to pull himself together and make a serious business of the leadership of this Party he will need to make them fall silent again and again. It isn't difficult for an intelligent man with a sharp tongue but it requires trouble and it requires House of Commons politics. And unfortunately Mr Jenkins, unlike Michael Foot for all his present dolorous condition, unlike Enoch Powell, unlike the Prime

Minister, unlike Norman Tebbit, is not someone who enjoys the Commons. He comes late, he does not stay long. If heckled (and he has invited heckling by sitting near the Hooligans), he does not fight back, and moreover he has shown a depressing tendency to ask a limp question, have it knocked down and then subside. When making a full speech he has run no risks and won no rewards.

There is a Buxton Spa style there, as of a man who had to become leader but has no appetite for leading. Jenkins is a man to whom one's reactions vary. He lacks the strong vein of ill-nature which powers Edward Heath. He does have a sense of humour; his books on Dilke, Asquith and Edwardian politics are exceedingly readable. His is a high intelligence and not a dogmatic one. His views on the economy and, one suspects, on Europe, have been modified by experience. He even used to be a good speaker, something which he may yet, like King David surrounded by 630 maiden-surrogates, warm to again. But he is the victim of his early success. That he should have risen, given both his talents and membership of an honourable Labour aristocracy as the son of Arthur Jenkins— Member of Parliament and PPS to Mr Attlee—was inevitable. Incidentally the customary abuse that he has betrayed the workers/the Welsh/the cause, by his donnish tastes and moderate views, betrays an ignorance of the aspirations of industrial workers with a chance of becoming something else, and of the improving, education-preoccupied outlook of old-fashioned union leaders. There is nothing inherently wrong with Balliol, what is at fault is Balliol overkill.

Like Shirley Williams he was praised too soon and too much for his own good. There were cooing little reports of 'the sought-after dinner parties' which he and his wife gave in the right part of North Kensington. And as the cameras nuzzled closer they drew out vanity. A 1966 Sunday feature entitled 'The Tolerant Community' showed a photograph of Jenkins leaning across his desk with fingertips pressed caringly together. The illusion of the phrase, the mannerism of the picture, did not make people laugh then as such phrases and mannerisms make people laugh today. He was given star treatment, partly because the owners of newspapers have a horror of the Labour Party's Left and because many of those writing for them found his Rousseau phase delightful. If you could have believed the newspapers, and you never can, there was only one possible successor to Harold Wilson—Roy Jenkins. Popularity in the press of course creates jealousy but it is not fatal to a politician who also takes good care to be popular with those who will have to choose the leader.

But why did this angel, seconded to the Labour Party by orders from the heavenly authorities, come to be so cruelly rejected and cast out? The Labour Party in Parliament which did the choosing in the prologue to the 1976 leadership election was consistently what is loosely and confusingly called 'right-wing', and Jenkins actually wore the uneasy coronet of deputy leader. Yet he finished up with a miserable total of fifty-four votes. Jim Callaghan, a low, cunning politician strong on simulated good nature, a hack, a machine politician and a man of distinctly reactionary views, walked into the job. Yet no one was seriously surprised. Callaghan is a very good hack, a first-rate machine politician and he is above nothing, especially not the cultivation of the Parliamentary Party. The successful politicians—Harold Wilson, Jim Callaghan, Margaret Thatcher—have all been those willing to stoop and determined to conquer. Unimportant obscure Members can always count on recognition, conversation, small kindnesses.

Jenkins was always incapable of flesh-pressing, Lyndon Johnson politics even in microcosm. Either he is shy and seems aloof or he is aloof and seems shy. For whichever reason, he retreated, like Hugh Gaitskell, to the friends of his choice. But where Gaitskell, a Wykehamist with thirties ideals, liked working-class Members and in an angular sort of way showed warmth to industrial workers, Jenkins was far too close to them to feel any such thing. Instead, he gathered around him a group of intelligent, socially neutral or up-market people who responded with devoted loyalty which never contained enough criticism or stimulation. At the end in a party of 320 there were 54 people who adored and a rather larger number who did not greatly care for him. Also, with what looks like the most crashing folly, he had actually tried to cultivate *upwards*. The friendships with the editor of *The Times* and the proprietor of the *Observer* and, through his historical work, with the Asquith and Bonham-Carter family connection, mattered too much for a man who wanted to be leader of the Labour Party. Labour has always been, until very lately, a very tolerant Party with a handful of agreeable aristocratic elements mingling with the representatives of industrial workers and with the exam-passers who wanted the best jobs, on a basis of friendly dislike. But while sycophancy towards the inheriting element, the cringe which comes naturally, has been a major part of Conservative politics (and especially of the One Nation, God Bless Queen Anne element) it is not a wise way to seek advancement in the Labour Party.

There was something else. He is capable of working very hard and capable of losing all interest. His first period at the Home Office, however chichi, had some good things in it and he was in his very Tory way, able to get away with being a thoroughly provident, money-watching Chancellor. His second term at the Home Office, when his British ambitions were receding and the sweets of Belgium tempting, was half-hearted, lackadaisical and apathetic. He could not be bothered.

Now the qualities of Jenkins in the Labour Party are no different to the qualities of Jenkins in the SDP. Its real constituency is very select but rather small. It is dear to a large part of the British establishment which wants Esau rather than Jacob; and this is Esau's party all right. 'Behold, Esau my brother is a hairy man and I am a smooth man.' And because England is a country with a huge bump of deference, in 1981 and early 1982 they nearly got the show right off the ground. As they now stand quarrelling on a narrow rock in a high sea as to which former office-holder shall take precedence in this narrow escarpment, they have inflicted an absurdity upon themselves. Old quarrels and pettinesses have spilt over from Party I to Party IA.

Shirley Williams, an immense television asset, is at odds with Jenkins, partly because she is rather more radical (or meddlesome), and partly because they are in conflict for the same caring, media constituency.

Williams is another victim of too much love from the press, some of it given because she was well wired up, some because she has the art of political attractiveness. Margaret Thatcher will never speak as well on television. Her impulse to tell the microphone to pull itself together is too great. Mrs Williams by contrast frequently wears *her* microphones in bandoliers like a Balkan sharpshooter. And she murmurs into them. Her reasonable, fair-minded voice never proclaims that her Party (whichever one it is) has a hundred per cent of the political wisdom. It might, she suggests, be over-ambitious to suggest 70 per cent, but they are fundamentally trying to get it right. Surely it would be a bit churlish not to vote for a Party whose spokesman is reasoning with us in such a grown-up way and making so few brassy slogans. You can trust Shirley. It is all a very subtle slogan to itself. She is a wonderful salesman. If it doesn't work too well in the Commons that is because it is the hardest market of all to sell in—sales resistance arranged neatly in rows of unbelieving males in the same trade. And even there, while she is brought down to earth and her reputation thought vastly overdone, she could if she organized a big push—First World War style—get things going.

The trouble with Mrs Williams is very First World War—shell-shock. The defeat, by a modest Conservative candidate in a seat she had held for fifteen years without trouble, losing a 9,000 majority after having done the national promotion as television link-up and face-over, hit her. And I doubt if even the champagne-bath victory of Crosby has wholly put right the effects of defeat at Hertford and Stevenage. Certainly she wouldn't have joined the SDP without it. She is cautious; and despondency, together with the lack of anything to lose, brought her into an enterprise she would have avoided as long as she was on the fairway. As the new party seems to have ended up with its ball on the down slope of a bunker, she is not playing her natural game. So agitation is combining with squabbles over protocol to damage her talents. She is petulant and erratic, her squabbling within the group weighing down the virtues on display. It should also be said that while Jenkins has foolish affectations (one of his mannerisms, a quite agonizing curving over of the hand inwards from the wrist, suggests nothing so much as a leg-spin bowler loosening up before play), he is very shrewd and ministerially capable. Williams *per contra* has every stylistic virtue together with a certain sympathy for the bottom of the heap but she was never able to take quarter adequate control of a Ministry. And some of the agitation comes from self-doubt as well as the Hertford shrapnel blast.

She needs serenity, and at the moment she doesn't have it. Yet with all her limitations she is the one important SDP politician with a common touch or indeed with common sympathy.

This is not to praise her integral talent. She has perhaps a fifth of Jenkins's intelligence but substitutes for the power of a mind the instincts of a natural if depressive politician. She can go out and get herself liked. It is not a contemptible talent in a Party so many of whose members flinch from human contact.

Dr Owen and William Rodgers have very little in common except a certain grandeur of manner. Rodgers is an underrated man but partly through his own fault. He actually enjoys being a henchman and instinctively avoids trying to come top of any bill. There is a faint air of Jeeves and Bertie in his relationship with Jenkins. He is a moderate speaker but he hustles wonderfully, like Jeeves shimmering round a room full of Party regulars at speed but with the sort of civility which makes them all feel they have been picked out. But he is actually at his best on hard facts and details, something which gave him a very good name at the Ministry of Transport. And indeed he needs rather badly to use his gifts. Preoccupation with in-fighting, and especially the in-fighting which the operatic personality of Mrs Williams helped precipitate, has wasted a good deal of his time. Bill Rodgers has always held the sound Tory view that knives were for private use.

Possibly David Owen understands something of the Party's lost directions. His candidacy against Jenkins at first seemed vain, conceited and selfish. So it was. But it did not retain its first appearance of futility. Owen in the Commons is the one SDP speaker to have carved for himself, and to have won, unloving but dispassionate respect from Labour and the Conservatives. He got the Falklands right and got them right in a voice which carried. His speeches didn't sound like the limp utterances of a political jelly baby. He is going to be re-elected. And with the exception of Robert MacLennan, who represents an unusual Scottish highland constituency where he has a lot of friends, Owen may be the only SDP member who can feel confident of doing that.

Above all Owen is not tired like Jenkins, neurotic like Williams or parliamentarily diffident like Rodgers. He pays the Commons the compliment of coming and speaking. And he is quite formidable, instinctively aggressive, not asking to be liked, which is wise, but trying to bring a bit of percussion to reinforce the murmuring woodwind trio of his colleagues. One does not feel warmth for the man. Being talented enough to be a surgeon and getting into the House in his twenties and the Foreign Office at 39 would create notions of grandeur in meeker souls than David Owen. But his superiority does not keep him above the fight. He goes down on to the floor with all those dreadful people against whom Jenkins seems to be holding a cloved orange to his nose, and he fights.

The other ranks of Social Democracy contain talent, but with the noted exception of George Cunningham whom the Social Democrats don't deserve, it is generally talent to fill office up to the rank of Junior Minister. One looks at the four figures mentioned earlier: John Roper, Ian Wrigglesworth, Tom Bradley and John Cartwright, all in the career structure of orthodox politics at or just on the edge of junior office, and contrasts them with four figures taken from Labour's younger men—Robin Cook, Frank Field, Jack Straw and Jeffrey Rooker—and there is simply no comparison. The Labour four are cleverer, more vital, have more beliefs, more energy. They may be identified with policies which ought not to be enacted. No 'maybe', they are! But they are also superior specimens with blood in their veins and ideas in their heads. Jenkins for the most part gathers to him dull, subordinable men. John Horam is better than this. With George Cunningham and the quiet but immensely well-briefed Bruce Douglas-Mann, he made up the only potential front-bench talent which the four great ones took with them. Mike Thomas should have been another but he seems to have lost heart. Horam on the market economy is worth listening to. No man who, in his apprentice days in marketing, invented the After Eight mint as the most expensive way of selling chocolate and got away with it, should be underestimated. And the terrible trouble with the SDP is that although it will be lucky to have five seats in the next Parliament, it is not equipped or disposed to be an effective Opposition Party. And they made the mistake of extreme elaboration of their policies, including Regional Governments and Assemblies. In cricketing terms they moved off the coconut matting of what they were *against* on to the violently turning wicket of what they were *for*.

There really are returns for a rational civility in politics, for the unfaked, lowered voice of reasonable argument. If, instead of playing at Governments, they had bothered, if they had tried, even with the limited talents they have, to involve themselves heavily in Parliament, to speak more, as an Opposition, it would have spilled over into their standing in the country. Parliament is so much more important than it seems. Not often does one fail there and succeed elsewhere. And the SDP, limp, somnambulant, respectful in the ranks towards their frayed pettish leaders, does fail.

The Liberals start with the advantage of having been a minority Party in opposition for longer than the lifespans of any of their Members excepting only Mr Grimond who was born when the last Liberal attempt at coalition was still contributing to its own destruction. Their broad parliamentary membership is rather more interesting than the SDP's.

Alan Beith is a good deal more important to the Party than he is taken to be, has grown from a slightly gawky manner to a dry and humorous one, while doing a lot of the work. Untidy black hair sits above an amiably academic face dominated by black-rimmed glasses. The manner is that of an academic gone to the good.

Stephen Ross, currently engaged in drawing the Home Secretary's attention to the broad corruption of the City and Metropolitan Police Forces, would, without the bad health which punishes him, be a substantial force. Ross, a tall, ungainly man always appearing to be in imminent danger of falling over, has a marked vein of courage. The Liberal assembly (in contrast with the Parliamentary Party), is full of people who hate the Atlantic Alliance, effective defence and, given the chance, capitalism itself. Ross as occasional Defence spokesman has the tribulations Labour spokesmen used to have before that Party surrendered to its militants and gave up defence. Ross, facing up to the subject before an unhappy Assembly audience, showed a nice balance of lucidly put facts, courtesy to his opponents and want of equivocation. He spoke in a way that one remembers. He is perhaps not an outstanding politician, but there is a flavour of good nature and sense which carries better than that of more flamboyant headline promoters. He is not particularly big in Parliament, but unlike the running footmen of the SDP, he gets respect and interest.

The other surprising strength among the Liberals, against all expectations, has been David Alton. Most very young politicians are insufferable either from arrogance or priggishness. At first one would have painlessly docketed Alton into the second category. Typically for the more righteous sort of politician he is small; he is intense, he wishes to do good. One feared for the worst. Then along came the Toxteth riots, in or abutting Alton's constituency (a seat taken, to their rage, from Labour). Alton was present for much of the trouble. He is a single-mindedly conscientious MP and wouldn't otherwise have won the seat. It can be said with some certainty that he knows what he is talking about. And at a time when almost the whole of the political nation, the *civitas dei* of politics, was in open-bowelled panic before the just and avenging looters and street thieves, Alton effectively got up and said 'I was there. The riots were criminal acts. It is fatuous to talk about "dialogue" when that will mean a dialogue with thieves and looters.'

Alton did more than make brave speeches in the midst of all this. He was an eyewitness and, with his local knowledge, an expert witness, and he went clean against the high-toned Jello fashion of the Scarman report. The Liberals have a name for limp-wristedness and feebleness; nobody can accuse David Alton of contributing to it. He seems to comprehend Liverpool for the hell above water which history, geography, subsidy and frightened Governments have made it. He also beat a left-wing socialist in a working-class seat. Shome lesshion here for the Sh.D.P. I think.

Most of the other Liberals are unremarkable. One could talk about Mr Wainwright's drab little disquisitions on the economy but not if one can avoid it. A plump man with the manner of a paternalist mill owner, he says the things which Peter Shore and Ian Gilmour say, and President Mitterrand used to say, about the benefits of non-inflationary reflation. He is without real harm in him but is one of the nags of Parliament and very good business for the tea-room.

Russell Johnston, who represents Inverness and speaks the crystalline, shaming English of that city, is a nice man, nobody's enemy and a gentle Christian soul who might have the qualifications for taking up the holy chalice which Wagner reserved for the holy fool. Johnston is one of that handful of friends of the EEC who actually believe in it, not because it was yesterday's wisdom and one of the thistles lining the route to a Junior Minister's office. Still less was he one of the looters of Europe. He has sought no mink-lined job in Brussels, no seat in the 'parliament' without powers in which a man can save his salary and live on expenses. Johnston just thinks that nations should come together and trust one another, that the hundreds of millions we lost are compensated for by the joy of giving and the greater good of the community. Johnston, bless him, actually complained when Mrs Thatcher banged M. Giscard's head against the kerb to get a little of our money back. He thinks that we should hold a billion pounds well lost if it pays for the privilege of belonging to 'Europe'. He goes everywhere surrounded by a pale light and there is nothing any ordinary low politician can do against him.

There is a myth that David Steel, the Microchap, is some sort of scrupulous idealist who has ventured into politics only out of a distasteful sense of duty. His steady rating, according to the slightly erratic Gallup company, hovers around 64 per cent approval—twelve points above Mrs Thatcher at the height of the

Falklands expedition. For someone who is shadow Home Secretary
in an Administration which will not be formed, this is rather good.

It occurs because Steel, like Shirley Williams, has the gift when on
television of underplaying, of soft speech, of quiet restraint. There
is no Tory politician in sight with this talent. The art lies in painting
high-tensile metal a delicate pastel shade, rose or powder blue.
Steel, quite rightly, does not want to go on being the leader of a
Ruritanian political party. His active members value their purity
and the fact is that the Liberals float some way above politics. Many
of them see their Party as a combination of beatification and golf, an
elevated, high-principled hobby which should not be soiled with
office. But Steel, a distinctly hard little man, means to make office
and if this means selling off grandmas, they go to the auction
rooms.

His chief achievement has been to create the SDP. It is
unimaginable that Jenkins would have been stirred from his
complacent, self-regarding early old age without the coaxing of the
man who had sedulously cultivated his friendship over many years.
It is a slightly Renaissance piece of intrigue. Steel believed that by
such an alliance the Liberal Party's cardinal defect, an inability to get
past the line of credibility (crossing which would give them the
difference between 12 and 150 seats under the British electoral
system) could be beaten. An organization doubled in size, with
some famous names added, could convey to the voter its capacity
for being elected and thus by self-firing logic be elected.

Steel, unlike the SDP, tries to keep away from policies. As he
understands, they make enemies or are not understood by your
candidates or they provoke splits. Shrewdly he has tried to
concentrate on the merits of what he is not. Nobody gives a bone
button for co-ownership, but they like nice moderate people. They
also like new faces in office without the menace of something
dangerous actually being done. Personality and image are what
matter. In this Steel is ahead of British politics, much closer to the
American model. He does not concern himself excessively with
minutiae but rather with projection, concentrating on a broad
affability and blandness which will catch votes. To put it brutally, if
Jenkins was any good, Steel might have brought it off. Alas, he is
not dealing with a fighting soldier of politics but with a Grand
Duchess in a litter. He wants, by means of support in a coalition, to
buy from the feebler Tories the Proportional Representation which
would destroy them but which, in the manner of the Foreign Office
giving away some strategic colony, some of them are quite capable
of granting.

One has to be impressed by Steel. There is no great intellect there
and no driving ideas. The personality, though very strong, is kept
sheathed and bears no relationship to the fellow borrowed from the

nativity play who takes part in TV discussions. And consider, he had on his hands at the start a political Party whose previous leader had felt the fingers of the police on his collar. One will not trouble a publisher's libel lawyer by describing Mr Jeremy Thorpe, but the Liberals did survive the only allegation that one can recall of attempted murder against the leader of a British political Party made for some little time. It was a nightmarish affair, especially in such a *douce* little Party, like the Mafia descending on Harrogate. Yet there they are still, intact, with the usual quota of a dozen or so seats and actually indulging in the luxury of wondering whether in mixing with the 'machine politicians' who can be found in the SDP they are not corrupting their image.

Steel being Steel kept his nerve and saw them through. His ambitions for a central coalition will fail, and what possible utility they would have if they were to succeed is not clear. But one has to admire the inspired *Zwergenpolitik* which has come interestingly close to turning a hobby Party into part of a grand coalition of state.

For Steel, unlike any other Liberal, including the delightful Jo Grimond, is actually a politician, a calculator, someone trying to win. Even in his early days as a reformer in the sixties he was shrewd. It wasn't terribly clever politically of the Wilson Government to weaken the penal system as it did. Homosexual law reform was just, but very far from popular, and only an unambitious politician (Leo Abse) could have promoted it. Steel chose abortion!

The friendship of Steel and Jenkins is a thing brought about when some necessary, some foolish and some malign legislation was being enacted in the meretricious mid-sixties. Jenkins wanted admiration from the best people; Steel wanted, from a much humbler political rank, to achieve power. Ironically, Steel, who has the cold talent to advance, is yoked by choice with a sacred but enfeebled beast who, having created wonders by his reappearance, has turned into a burden. Steel's hard little face conceals, as best it can, the tragedy which follows from making—like his predecessor—an unwise choice of company.

5

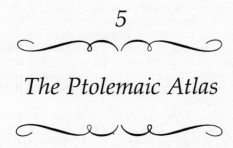

The Ptolemaic Atlas

The phrase is Mr John Biffen's, and he used it to speak dismissively of the concepts of 'Right' and 'Left' within the Parties or across the spectrum. 'Defining anything as "Right" or "Left"', he said, 'is like trying to find your way on a Ptolemaic Atlas.'

Interestingly, other words have been substituted as if they too meet a need. Labour speaks usefully of its Hard Left and Soft Left, the Conservatives, since the terms 'Wet' and 'Dry' appeared, have spun off enough meteorological metaphors to sustain a cottage industry. Oddly, the term 'Wet' was first generally used by Mr Edward Heath to describe persons flinching from policies he thought necessary.

But the present division between Dries and Wets relates to the economy. A Dry believes in the free market, opposes state intervention, dislikes subsidies, believes in control of the money supply and as his first priority, wants inflation brought down. He does not rejoice at unemployment but he regards past inflation as being among its principle begetters. He is also an enemy of the strong state, of all forms of corporate power, of regulations in restraint of trade. He holds such views not only because he does not think corporate power good for a strong economy, but, morally, because it has concentrated power with civil servants and the sharper Ministers, has diminished Parliament by means of a wealth of quasi-autocratic powers and has developed that gradualist authoritarianism so well expressed in the passive impersonal formation 'it is thought that'. Wets and Dries are united in their apprehensions about freedom. But Wets believe that freedom is threatened from below—by riots, by Mr Arthur Scargill and, in their

78

darker moments, by the just revenge of the working class. The Dries fear the authority of the Ministerial circular broadening down from generation to generation, the Board of Intrusion with its statutory powers, the threat to freedom from above.

Wets have been rather wrong-footed. They had been brought up to believe that the only hope for the Conservative Party's survival lay in being and seeming to be compassionate, in spending great sums of money from general revenue, while uniting with all other Conservatives about the need for the rich to stay rich. The Wet position is a fascinating combination of Keynes, Christianity and panic. It has been scared of almost everything except inflation. It believes that the pain of unemployment can be significantly alleviated by 'selective and non-inflationary reflation', though M. François Mitterrand has met with some difficulties in doing this. The best of them are sincerely moved by the miserable fact of unemployment and would simply like to do something about it. The worst of them look back to the convictionless, meretricious world of Mr Macmillan as a May Ball into which the tradesmen have intruded.

Most of the standard ideas which are called 'Wet' have to do with keeping people in their places. The devotion to Disraeli, the masonic handshake of the fraternity, is a terrible admission of intellectual dereliction. In so far as that multiple bankrupt poseur had any convictions at all, they did not constitute the idea of 'One Nation' but of a grateful peasantry securely reigned over and provided with nutritious scraps by the inhabitants of 'Great Houses' at which Disraeli would be a continuously circulating house guest. The genius of Benjamin Disraeli was to have told the hereditary aristocracy that they were nicer than they were. Not nice, just nicer.

Most of politics has to do with fear or self-advancement, and in the fifties the Tories, recovering from the shock of the Labour landslide, were attracted to an orthodoxy which suggested that they could keep much more of the old world than they had expected, providing that, out of economic growth, the workers took enough to keep them happy. And if there wasn't enough economic growth the workers had better take it anyway. There would be problems but they would come later. This new inflation business was a bother and might have to be subjected to a short squeeze, provided that was swapped for a spot of selective, non-inflationary reflation in good time for the general election. Thus did Mr Macmillan institutionalize fecklessness, not in people but in governments.

Fecklessness was also kin with fear. Among some of the Wets there is a large element of jittery apprehension about losing what they have. I can never listen to Sir Ian Gilmour, arch-castigator of the Government and owner of a useful part of Middlesex, without hearing the words 'Father, father, the men are coming up the drive.'

If you have a lot to lose, all policies which can remotely be called tough (and the Government is not very tough) are frightening. The men may make trouble. The institutional Conservative Party, so much more important than any grubby idea, may be damaged.

Of course, with the Labour Party in its present depressing state, there is nothing stupid in wanting to keep the other lot out, but the attitude produces a sterility of mind, an imitative quality. Much of what was really wrong in the Heath years derived from the preceding historical hostility to ideas and the consequent immediate need to grab at anything which could pass for one. One thinks, without pleasure, of the reorganization, as it was called, of local government and of the Health Service.

Now, the grand futilities of the NHS and the local government reorganization are acknowledged. With typical scruple, Sir Keith Joseph (who was at Health) has admitted that he was wrong, as, typically, Mr Walker has not. A character formed in the harder edges of the City can be lacquered but not altered. But the real fault lay not in the Ministers themselves half so much as in the habit of mind which says 'We are a Government. Governments do things. What complex, elaborate, futile thing should we do?' The laws thus created are elaborate, for folly is a many-scheduled thing. If you are very lucky they are no worse than wholly useless. Probably they will create false jobs, which being unproductive, are a direct public debt and a contribution to the slowly accumulating state of affairs which ends in exceptionally high interest rates and the loss of real jobs. They are simply a substitution of the simulated for the real. The negative men, anxious to be in office but unaware of the many great glories of inactivity, not only inflict this kind of political basket-weaving upon themselves, they commonly, if unconsciously, defer much more than they realize to the orthodoxies of the Left.

The Left has never, in a radioactive way, been short of ideas. And vacuums have a way of being filled. So the entire Conservative Party in Parliament went on dead march through the lobbies to carry Mr Heath's Industry Bill—a piece of permissive power to intrude and intervene and to spend unauditable money which enabled his Labour successors to act without further legislation, merely using the peremptory powers kindly provided by a Conservative Government. If one thinks of politics as a parallelogram between Left and Right rather than two fixed wings, then the preoccupation with the business of being 'in' can rapidly create a leftward-leaning parallelogram. This is the only sense in which the terms Left and Right have much relevance. So when one hears a certain kind of Conservative, hostile to monetary theories, complaining, he is oddly enough lamenting a state of affairs in which, however extensive the problems, the Conservatives have found themselves initiators. In spite of the current militancy of the Far Left within Labour, we are not too far from the prospect of a rightward-leaning parallelogram. Indeed Mr Peter Shore, for all his fierce debating style, is only offering the country a hotter version of what Sir Ian Gilmour would like to offer—selective non-inflationary reflation.

The business of not thinking but doing, of filling the hours provided with proof to the electorate that one is a real, tiresome, law-passing, order-in-council-making, damn nuisance of a Government is not confined to Conservatives. It is part of the larger orthodoxy of what are called moderate politics. Moderate politicians know very clearly what they are against, but they will never be content with the wisdom of putting nothing in its place. It is absolutely no surprise to find the SDP in one of its green papers proposing another reorganization of local government, which for meddling hyper-activity makes Mr Peter Walker look like Parson Woodforde. In imitation (and imitation is always about wherever there is moderation) of the West Germans, they wish to create a dozen provincial authorities—not just a new tier of local government (too commonplace an atrocity) but a dozen Regional Parliaments, each with its Regional Government and its Regional Prime Minister.

In a stupor-inducing way the whole psychology of moderation is fascinating. Mr Heath, normally so infelicitous with the English language, can be credited with launching the word 'moderate' into general and recurring use in his last months in power. Mr Arthur Scargill was the bug-eyed monster of the day and clearly not a moderate man. It is a splendid word which no one should be without. 'Right-Wing', quite apart from its general meaninglessness, carried connotations of Lt.-Colonels Rtd., who thought that the country was going to the dogs. The implications of 'Right' were old fashioned, Blimpish, *ancien jeu*. No advertising agency, from Colman, Prentice and Varley to Saatchi and Saatchi, would advise in favour of it. It did Mr Heath no good, this sudden flush of verbal aptitude. The entire November 1974 election was spent by Conservative spokesmen urging in the most nebulous terms their moderation and their willingness to do anything which a coalition partner asked them to do in the name of moderation. One has never seen a political Party in such a state of prideless self-abjection. What it offered was less of a manifesto than a colouring book. And it lost.

On parallel, if less humiliating, lines Sir Harold Wilson's view of politics, afflicted as it was by the unspoken despair which seems to be one of the occupational hazards of the job, led him into all sorts of trifling shadow play. For the moderate wing of the Labour Party was again clearest about what it did *not* want. And it is a most creditable list. They did not want unilateral nuclear disarmament. With a brave and dogged Foreign Secretary in Michael Stewart, they did not want the triumph of the North Vietnamese. Nor did they favour nationalizing the means of production, distribution and exchange, nor the break-up of the Atlantic Alliance, nor the sort of power in the hands of the trade unions which they were themselves gloomily to bestow after 1974. In all of this, they were in no conflict with the electorate but horribly embarrassed with their own membership. Not surprisingly such politicians turned to issues like devolution with the same delight as did those Conservatives who belonged to the moderate orthodoxy. It was painless, elaborate, radical-seeming and interminable, the perfect pre-definition of a moderate policy. That it was also wasteful, bureaucratic, either meaningless or constitutionally explosive was totally irrelevant. It bought off trouble and it created a tremendous amount of solemn activity. But (and this very well illustrates how confusing the Ptolemaic Atlas is) devolution, the supreme example of moderate policy-substitute, the acorn coffee of the middle ground, was not broken by the Left. They, surprisingly, have their own streak of comforting defeatism in that they like being betrayed and wouldn't feel happy otherwise. It was defeated by members of what might be called the Independent Tendency.

The cause which can summon up the concerted opposition of George Cunningham, Bruce Douglas-Mann, Tam Dalyell, Nick Budgen, Teddy Taylor, and Iain Sproat is up against trouble, but is hardly facing a narrow, concerted world view. What such Members have in common is a bump of independence. Cunningham, Taylor and Dalyell in particular are the sort of people who make whips wake up screaming. If they think that the broad drift of responsible opinion, with *The Times* and all men of goodwill united behind it, is wrong, they will throw rocks. Sometimes they will get a little wild, as Tam Dalyell did in his brave, mistaken one-hander against the Falklands expedition, but such men also learn to be very cunning with procedure. We were saved from a piece of futilitarian nonsense by the George Cunningham 40 per cent amendment, which changed the entire psychology of expectations in the Scottish Referendum, and by Teddy Taylor, who talked the Tory shadow cabinet round from the position of functional coalition with the Government on this issue to one of strenuous and clear opposition which mobilized the Scottish Tory vote. Yet many of these admirable wreckers are naturally moderate men.

Douglas-Mann, the Social Democrat casualty at Mitcham and Morden, was, his courage only excepted, precisely the sort of mild, humane, reforming person one would expect to see in the SDP. Such 'moderates' gleefully joined in with the rough boys from the extremist comprehensive up the road in an escapade which right-thinking people can only condemn. In other words, the presence of personality is a factor which distinguishes one sort of politician from another.

There are natural regimental men (not necessarily creeps, their own special and delectable species) who are the nationalists of party, the patriots of the line. They will exalt a leader as the one without fault or reproach until the consensual moment of his or her urgent dispensability is reached. The regimental politician is neither Wet nor Dry, Right nor Left, Hard nor Soft. He is a stampede empiricist for whom a policy's broad ability to keep the Party strong is the measure of its utility. Such men are also affected by the quality of a leader. There are men whose views run rather contrary to those of the Prime Minister but who are most loyal supporters, precisely because the regiment has found itself a colonel who takes command and wins battles . . . as long as she does.

But, paradoxically, the way in which, by chance and with her hand forced, Mrs Thatcher found herself finally ascendant within her Party was one which the most illiberal bookie would have offered 200 to 1 against—a reassertion of the values of the Old Right. (The words 'Right' and 'Left' do insist on cropping up from time to time.) The Old Right, quite unlike the Dries, takes a stoical view of the economy as something which neither they nor anybody else properly understands. They admire the Dry and deflationary position only for the horrendous courage which it takes to sustain, but they are devoted to things which are above economics. The Old Right has been mocked with inexpensive facility. For it tends to care about patriotism, the Queen, England, the Armed Forces and the flag.

It is as far, from various different angles, from the viewpoint of Mr Roy Jenkins as from that of Mr Reg Race or for that matter of Mr Jock Bruce-Gardyne. It believes in its own bloodstream, and until April 1982 it was considered an absurdity, a territory inhabited by headless dragons like Mr Winston Churchill. Indeed the quality of its membership has always been a defect. Taking Mr Julian Amery seriously, when he has retained a style of address which would have excited no comment sixty years ago, is difficult; likewise the study in pink and black which is Sir Bernard Braine. But then so many opportunities occur in life to quote Melbourne's remark about all the damn fools being right and all the clever fellows wrong that those of us who had slipped into the habit of being patronizing should have known better. For the Old Right is not only not as stupid as it insists on sounding, it is often quite expert. With a number of Members for naval constituencies, it gave Sir John Nott's airily unchallengeable decisions on the need to phase out the Navy a strenuously combative time.

It was the instinct of the Old Right which asserted itself on the

Saturday sitting on 3 April 1982. People like Sir Bernard Braine and Mr Patrick Cormack discovered an ability to hijack foreign policy which most people dismissed as the merest taking and driving away, simple joy-riding, but which ended at the other end of the planet. Now most of the Labour Polytechnic Left do not even bother to hate and despise such people. Which is why the Polytechnic Left got such a nasty shock. They had been so totally preoccupied with hating and despising the monetarists, whom they regard as serious people, that the idea of any threat coming from the heirs and assigns of Sir Walter Bromley-Davenport was just too preposterous.

The reason why the Old Right dominated the scene was in part because the Prime Minister, if not quite one of them, is distinctly High Church on the subject, but chiefly because the 'Country', a word which had been in serious danger of being dropped for 'Society', was violently of the same inclination. The working class frequently disappoints its rightful leaders. On this occasion it betrayed them shockingly. Even Mr Foot, not the most ept of men, grasped fairly quickly how the broad masses felt and toned down his response much more drastically than the unforgiving Tories gave him credit for.

The social case-workers and the polytechnicians were left too aghast and unbelieving to make any sort of a show. Real resistance, apart from whatever the Foreign Office may have been doing, came from Tam Dalyell with one or two obscure Members taking walk-on parts. Apart that is from Mr Heath, who long before the Task Force reached the Falklands, requested a turn-round back to Ascension Island on the grounds that by having sailed so far the Task Force had achieved its purpose.

But what mattered was the people, the vote-casting electorate, and notably the working-class section of it. One may say with some certainty that they were not against poor General Galtieri because he was alleged (inaccurately) to be a fascist. They were against him because he was a foreigner. They knew what they wanted and were not going to be denied. The refinements of those at the Foreign Office who had programmed themselves for painless evacuation of all positions held, the pre-occupation of the economic cast of mind with exchange rates and productivity, the desire of many rather acquiescent politicians of every persuasion to lead a quiet life, were all swept aside. As for an expression of the essential horror that a country in the West might fight for itself, beat an enemy and be proud of the fact, that had to wait for the Service of Thanksgiving. George Orwell remarked that of all the isms the one which had real staying-power was nationalism. 'Children play with tin soldiers. They do not', he said, 'play with tin pacifists.'

We were told that the Tory Party used to wrap itself in the flag, or, this being England and a decorous country, to employ it as a tablecloth for their platform meetings. Such brazen vulgarity was put behind us in the exhilaration of 'the dash for growth', 'Fanfare for Europe' and 'controlling M3'. We became, or just as important were declared to be, a 'civilized, caring, forward-looking, not to say multi-ethnic society'. Instead, to the amazement of everyone, from the Open University to Leopoldo Galtieri, we turned out to be a Country. Any political party might in principle enjoy the advantage of the patriotic wind if it had the disposition. And in this Tuscan landscape of undulations which is our political scene, there were significant front- and back-bench figures on the Labour side who were in total sincere empathy with the War Party. The speech of Mr Ken Weetch at a point when the Foreign Office seemed close to some kind of compromise is a case in point; and of course Mr Shore, who has a very English view of the world, took a similar if more private stand.

On the other hand there were Dry Conservatives who would say softly, 'It's happening and of course I have no alternative but to go along with it. Yet in my private heart I am a Cobdenite. I believe in trade and free markets and absolute political liberty and I am not terribly enthusiastic about enterprises which end with bodies in the water.'

This distinction between soldiers and traders, to use two unweighted and equally honourable words, is profound despite being unspoken. Though such is the confusion of our Ptolemaic Atlas that many, including the Prime Minister, belong to both categories.

Politics is also about being seen to be successful. No economic policy, not even the better-regarded ones like Mr Jenkins's stay at the Exchequer, really had them throwing roses from the circle and the gods. As a friendly whip of my acquaintance put it, 'Nothing works, my dear. Nothing ever does.' The war policy which wasn't sought and towards which the House itself concentrated and pushed the Prime Minister's mind that Saturday in April did have such an effect. For to a dispirited, much hectored, lectured-at nation the business of getting something of our own back and kicking the other fellow out with no guilt feelings at all was wonderful. It was of course possible for reasons which would appeal to the traders: good, utilitarian, economic reasons. The armed forces, unlike British Airways, the police and the economy, do more or less function. They are esteemed by other armed forces in a way that British Leyland is not esteemed by other motor companies. Reduced in size, but able to choose an elect of intelligent, brave young men and with some bits of equipment like the Sea Harrier, surely too good to have been made by the people we think we are, they represented that section of British life most likely to succeed. A dramatic critic once said that if there was a rifle slung over the

mantelpiece in the first act of a play, the only question was whether
it would be used to shoot somebody in the second or the third act.
The Navy may have been on the edge of terminal improvement by
Sir John but the general excellence of the forces was real. They were
also the way out of the enmiring defeatism (and defeat) which from
Disengagement East of Suez to Treaty of Accession to Mass
Unemployment have been our recent history.

Accordingly the Conservative Party in Parliament, returning to
an ancient style and posture and getting it more or less right, is
genuinely elated. For it has, with very little calculation, got on to the
wavelength of the people. The editor of the *Spectator* may wrinkle
his nose at a depressing exhibition of loud and disgusting jingoism.
But it is the editor of the *Sun* with headlines such as 'Gotcha', who is
in the business of guessing what a mass public actually thinks. That
is the unpleasant side to it. There is much coarseness of spirit on the
Old Right, but it is possible to argue that, quite apart from what has
been done for morale, the country, precisely because it did have
that coarseness, unthinkable to the German Federal Republic, the
press-oppressed Americans or any Western country (except of
course France), was able to win new standing in the world by doing
the unthinkable and doing it proficiently. Harold Macmillan, that
valetudinarian poseur, used to say that in relation to the United
States we must be Athens to Rome. There are those today who
would murmur 'What about Sparta?'

What is for sure is that the entire Conservative Party in
Parliament has acquired edge and bite. The old instinct to apologize
and explain that one is also as liberal and progressive as the other
chap, if not more so, has receded. We are at a point which must be
as nearly the polar opposite of the November 1974 election as could
be. Perhaps wrongly and in despite of economic anxieties, the
Conservatives have this feeling that their differences can all be
endured because they are influencing events.

Labour does not have this consolation; and Labour's differences,
always elaborate, have grown rococo as a quite different, losing-
side psychology takes over. Now it will no longer do to break
Labour into two simple categories. Part of their 'Old Right' (quite a
different *galère*) has got up and gone away to become the Social
Democratic Party. What remains has a certain decapitated chicken
quality about it, functioning as if all was as all used to be, and office
would mean the nice things it used to, and indeed as if office were a
strong possibility.

But those who have gone, breaking at least one mould as they
went, that of Labour unity, were, with one or two exceptions, the
passionate Europeans and the Friends of Roy Jenkins. The 'Right'
which remains differs from them over political judgement and over
that ever-recurring thing, Labour Party patrialism. 'This is my

party. I've always been in it. Yes, it's getting bloody awful, but I couldn't actually leave.' But as one of them put it to me, 'I'm not doing a Hattersley, saying that if the Labour Party introduces comprehensive infanticide, you get up and say "Well, that's a bit rough but, brothers, the Labour Party is bigger than all of us."'

Incredibly, there is still talent. Solid, brave men like George Robertson have a way of turning up. Their promotions are faster than they would have been, but the quality is still there. The residual Right still holds predominant office, but it is in what looks like fairly easy coalition with what is called the Soft Left. If you were trying to identify the Soft Left, you would of course find the tired militants, men grown mild under pressure, who had been good for a Conway Hall rant much of their lives, who have supported some strenuously foolish things in their time, who have perhaps in younger and happier days thought well of Uncle Joe and Uncle Ho without quite losing their innocence. Even so they are quite emphatically apart from the small Commons cell of Soviet-liners, men in perpetual mourning for Stalin. It would be unfair to tax the older members of the Soft Left with the cuttings job which could be done on the things they once said. They are tired and depressed. Jerusalem hasn't come, nor will it. They were in office with Jim Callaghan, and they have stayed there, most of them, instituting those cuts in public expenditure with which, in 1976, the present era of deflating the economy began.

Many of them are attractive, honourable men who have working-class origins and loyalties and whose triumphalist socialism has been worn and battered with the access of responsibility. No fair-minded man could dislike Stan Orme. Paradoxically, people like Mr Orme were at their most radical in the time of Hugh Gaitskell. Yet it is not unrealistic to see them voting for Peter Shore, whose prejudices come closer to those of Hugh Gaitskell than those of any man alive.

But the Soft Left is itself divisible. Orme and Kinnock represent a working-class tradition which is radical by affection and old fidelities but which finds itself able to work more closely to our lurching and swaying political status quo as represented by the Callaghan Government than ever it thought possible, and at the same time more depressed by the alsatian dogs of street and conference militancy.

People like Jack Straw, Frank Field and Robin Cook are different yet again because they are more middle class and have recently been more zealous than the others. They are the young men (Neil Kinnock, despite his inexcusable youth, belongs in some ways to the generation of men twenty years older). The disaffection of the Straws, Fields and Cooks with what Mr Benn has wrought could be put down cynically to a cool grasp of the limitless capacity of the

Benn doctrines for losing elections and keeping highly capable young men out of parliamentary Under-Secretaryships. It is rather better than that. Zealous they may be, millenarians they are not. Ultimately their distance from Bennism is a mixture of intelligence and distaste. They are not, like the elder part of the Soft Left, tired and depressed. They have their own radical intentions but see the Militant Tendency and the group of ardent, intense men around Tony Benn—Michael Meacher, Stuart Holland and, at a primitive level, Reg Race—as an infantile complaint, and, thus one which is good for an effective socialist Labour Party, the way disinfectant is good for the digestion. This faction which, given its propensity to think, might be called the Accelerated Fabians, is not dedicated to the nationalization of that four-fifths of the private sector still standing after the slump. Though they would be ardent regulators, price controllers and would have ideas about nationalized industries as pace-makers which, like Jeeves's definition of Nietzsche, would be 'radically unsound, sir'. The heaviest commitment of this sort of younger and sadder leftist is to welfare, to the lowest paid, to the Health Service. This is seen at its clearest in Frank Field, who increasingly impresses as a Christian radical of an old-fashioned and creditable sort. For him radical measures are attractive as a means to getting something done in a hurry, not as part of a seamless received truth. Field is an intense young man who actually *does* care passionately about a number of issues, notably the cause of those trapped in low incomes. Yet the affinity between Field, who is thought of as a left-winger, with the new coercionists, the scampering cell-mates of the Militant Tendency, is zero.

There *is* a Democratic Left; and perhaps it is fitting for a toiler at the *Telegraph*-face to say as much—it is essential to acknowledge them. The Accelerated Fabians make an intellectual judgement on the Hard Left, a gradualist's exasperation at the mood of Munster Anabaptism in the air. Their objection is not the straightforward politicianly one to anything which upsets the applecart. They have a distinct inclination to apply quality control to the apples. Such people are valuable, useful Members, people with ideas worth stealing. Their rejection of Mr Benn is the sternest judgement yet passed on him, for it effectively divorces him from that part of radical politics which can create things. If he had been able to keep them and adopt their ideas to his own, not only would he have had that useful affair, a majority, but that even more useful commodity, political intelligence.

There is a third facet to what the Soviets would call the rejectionist front, a group of MPs, many from the Midlands, concentrated around Jeffrey Rooker and Peter Snape, whose quarrel with Benn is a form of class war. Working class and sharp-elbowed themselves, they have conceived neither despair nor exasperation at the

Member for Bristol South-East but a derisive personal dislike. They see him as a dude, a mission curate practising street slang and at the same time a gentleman taking a gentleman's naturally assumed place of leadership. They reckon, not unreasonably, to know a thing or two about the working class, and Benn's disquisitions on it affect them like a rash. They are by conviction of an old, levelling disposition and not terribly respectful to anyone. They are nodody's yeomen—about the furthest point in personality from the sort of coterists who sustain Mr Jenkins. Their feeling about Benn is that of leather-jacketed method actors towards Beerbohm Tree.

Jeff Rooker is worth following. At the moment he is heavily underrated in the press. It remembers his unlucky blunder over the wholly unjustified allegation of corruption on the part of a director of British Leyland. The apology that Rooker was obliged to make by personal statement in the House was interestingly composed. The apology to the man named, Mr Frank Turner, was categorical and obviously meant; that to the company itself was tempered. Those elder, wiser figures in the gallery who dislike crude, *louche* characters have no time for Rooker. They have a feeling that he might improve with Borstal training. But they make a fundamental mistake. He has indeed a tone of heavy resentment and chips on both shoulders. But a Hooligan is what he *used* to be.

Rooker graduated from the bench of Hooligans as, briefly, did Bob Cryer. Unlike Cryer, who found adult company unbearable and climbed back into the play area, Rooker took to serious politics. And he did the work which is necessary for it. One afternoon he took on Patrick Jenkin, then at the DHSS. Jenkin is not exactly Spinoza, but he is a conscientious politician who handles his numbers with the facility of a former Treasury Minister. He quoted one set of figures. Rooker, who was opening the debate as the Opposition junior spokesman, let him become wholly committed to them. Then, making his own speech, he quoted some other, quite different sets of digits. Jenkin, a gentle, but agitatable personality, leapt up to say that Rooker's figures (they related to the earnings of low-wage groups after a tax adjustment) were wildly wrong, that the Honourable Gentleman 'was dwelling in the realms of fantasy'. 'Why', he added, a little naïvely, 'I have the Low Pay Unit's hand-out here.' 'I know', said Jeff, in his slow how-can-I-infuriate-you Birmingham accent. 'They're wrong!' He had spotted a mistake the night before, rung up the Unit and had the calculations redone and the error admitted.

Now a more gentlemanly politician might have notified his adversary, but there is nothing in *Erskine May* which requires politicians to be gentlemen. And the result was an outstanding parliamentary coup, the sort of thing which Rooker's old friends on the Hooligans' Bench are incapable of. Indeed, how often does one see a thoroughly competent Minister dropped out of a plane without a parachute? Rooker, five degrees milder in his style, is potentially a major figure on the Labour front bench. He has very much the same gift for mastering a subject while remaining a distinct personality which has made it possible for Norman Tebbit to move so swiftly, when office presented itself, from 'unspeakable creature, old boy' to 'candidly the strongest man we've got, my dear fellow'.

As for the True Left itself, well, we are out of Tuscany in landscape terms. One is not describing undulations but escarpments. Very roughly, there are two groups which matter: Mr Benn's following, and the Old Left. They tend to be older men, but new recruits come along like Screaming Ron Brown. There are, anyway, one or two younger men willing to defend the Soviet war against Afghanistan just as contributors to the *New Statesman* used to defend Stalin's show trials. A frequent approval of Soviet policies is much expressed only by Mr Frank Allaun, a great champion of peace, and Mr James Lamond. Mr Mikardo, always a manager rather than a boxer, says little these days and Miss Maynard plays no noisy part in politics. The chief verbal presence in this group is Norman Atkinson, for a number of years the Labour Party Treasurer, which tells one an eloquent amount about the state of the trade union delegate conferences.

Atkinson, tall, dark-haired and grudge-laden, has a manner which suggests that every injustice of capitalism, from the overseer's lash to the fourteen-hour day, had been personally inflicted on him. The same sour, world-hating spirit of a Michael Henchard, who had ended *The Mayor of Casterbridge* not by dying and asking 'that no man remember my name' but had gone into national politics, informs Mr Martin Flannery.

They are men at whose approach the milk of human kindness would turn into cottage cheese. Mikardo is no sweeter, but he has a vein of *bonhomie* so *fausse* that you could bottle and market it. The Baltic merchant has always enjoyed the promotion of other politicians. And, interestingly, he was an early advocate of Mr Benn's succession to power during that transitional phase when he was still Mr Wedgwood Benn the technologist and only barely discernible as being on the road to a collectivist Canossa.

The goodwill of the philo-Soviet group is always worth remembering in any contemplation of that very different and distinct gathering—Benn's People—who are not so compromised. The status of Lenin's useful idiots is never too far away. Benn himself is a first-rate speaker provided that he is not interrupted. He is constitutionally ill suited to thinking on his feet. What comes out is super-abundantly eloquent in a pattering fashion, but the reputation of being a major parliamentary figure is only partly deserved. If the Tory whips were half clever, which is asking a lot, they would arrange teams of informed back-benchers to rise and, with the civility of Castiglione, ask him as a very great favour, deeply appreciated, to help them with this or that purely factual question. It could wreak havoc; as it is, those interventions to which he has reluctantly given way he has usually regretted.

For the Benn group, though not without its lurking intelligences, Stuart Holland and, more impressively, Michael Meacher (who does have a great many figures at his finger ends) is happiest with conspiracy theories and thus much less effective in debate against the Government than Eric Varley, or John Smith, Labour's former Trade shadow. To suggest, not that the Government had got its figures wrong and thus stumbled into unemployment but that it delighted in the prospect and was seeking to smash the workers lacks credibility. The problem of this group is that its members have no overwhelming enthusiasm for Parliament and are obliged to function on a basis of occasional goodwill. In this Benn is rather like Mr Edward Heath. Time spent in the chamber is resented. The great man sits there patting the speech on his knee, exercising to the full the privilege of a Privy Councillor to be called ahead of the *Populo Minuto* on the back-benches proper. That speech is then made peremptorily and perfunctorily at some speed. Whether we are in our 'there-are-jobs-and-free-beer-for-all-on-Uranus' mood or something calmer, the speech is made without pleasure, and the man who made it lingers little or not at all thereafter. Both Benn and Heath tend to give us oratorio politics with the tenor looking irritably at his watch.

For what it is worth, the lower sort tend to go along with Mr Benn, Dennis Skinner, the Hooligan Royal, sometimes coming to consult with him, squatting in the middle of the gangway next to his favoured seat (third end above the gangway). Unlike Mr Benn, they actually *enjoy* Parliament and can't bear to be out of it. And there is no real affinity. The Hooligans with all their faults are flesh-and-blood football supporters beating the place up.

They recognizably belong to the other end of the same galaxy as the rest of us. Also, in a crude sort of way, they are Dantonists: resentful certainly, but also with a ragged flame of generosity. The close coterists of Benn have the marble touch of St Just. Michael Meacher, his chief asset, is a public school man with a sense of guilt and the manner of an embalmer's assistant.

One other distinction should be made after a tour of the spectrum—it may be greater than that between Left and Right, Dry and Wet, Hard and Soft—the good old distinction as wise as ten generations and a dozen ideologies, between In and Out. Not that we should limit the terms narrowly to Government and Opposition. There is, for a time, a touch almost of jollity about some of those relieved of office. Merlyn Rees for one became a new man. From the oppressed and nervous Home Secretary, head down behind his brief, always liable to snap or complain about the weight of the globe he was carrying, he has, since he got out, been a pleasure to watch—practically kissing babies out of election time. And for a couple of years he put on with Mr Whitelaw a courteous-Government-and-responsible-Opposition act which left those with ideas about Home Office reform feeling conspired against.

The Ins and Outs which really matter are to be seen in the same Party. Being Wet is after all largely a function of having expected somebody else to be Prime Minister. The most recent Wets can and do, with occasional intractable exceptions, adjust and keep their disapproval well within promotable limits. Those who held office or minor office or, saddest of all, shadow minor office, who have slipped from it and see no way back, are in a different case. It is a rotten time to be David Madel or Alan Haselhurst or indeed, among the unseeded, Hugh Dykes. You were or you were going to be. You are not and you don't look too much like ever being. On the whole they behave surprisingly well in the chamber, but a certain righteousness tends to get into their voices, virtue being the last refuge of the losing side.

Among the Tories, being Out for slightly more senior figures tends to produce an analytical approach to politics. They are blessed with three civil and creative critics in Peter Hordern, Terence Higgins and Peter Tapsell who are, if not enjoying their time by the Black Sea, at least turning out the *Metamorphoses*. They tend to make genuinely interesting, analytical speeches which are actually worth reading, not something one lightly says of a parliamentary speech.

Liberals and Social Democrats are of course, by definition, all Out. And virtue of a slightly acrid sort is everywhere apparent. They are preaching Parties, a little given to sonority and, even the youngest of them, to elder-statesmanship. Like the Bennites they can be Messianic, but it is Messianism with a spanner and an oilcan, preoccupied between pieties, mould-breakings and Ideas Whose Time Has Come, with ways of changing the electoral system so that more rather than fewer of them will be elected. This idealistic and passionate commitment to a guaranteed meal-ticket is a preoccupation which fits with the rest of the political landscape. It is merely chance that the *nice* people of politics are so placed by the electoral system that the low motives, which form part of every other faction's woodland and common, stand out for them rather more gauntly. As long as we remember that politics is about the deadly serious business of being, if not In then in with a chance, the refinements between groups, though very important, may, like all landscapes, acquire a perspective.

6

The Bomb Throwers

'He's my link with the bomb throwers.' The phrase was President Johnson's. The link was Hubert Humphrey, proof if you needed it that some of them are the nicest of fellows. There are two headings for back-benchers, 'Aspirants' and 'Bomb Throwers'. I propose to consider Bomb Throwers, leaving Aspirants for the tipster's list that follows.

Essentially, an Aspirant, even if he is a nice chap and good to his old mother, wants office. A Bomb Thrower only ever finds it by serendipity. By no means are all Aspirants creeps, though they do tend to hang around telephones during reshuffles. And while Bomb Throwers tend to be men of principle, the principle might well be an undying reverence for the Soviet Union or some other sincere conviction which makes Hattersley's cheerful cynicism almost endearing. The Bomb Throwers exist on both sides of the House, they overlap a little with the Hooligans, but it takes a far more serious caste of mind to be a Bomb Thrower than a Hooligan. The stance implies disrespect, a willingness to forgo self-advancement (in some cases a shrewd surrender of what was never on offer), and a disposition to drive a coach and four hobby-horses through the serenity of orthodox politics.

Speaking of hobby-horses, Leo Abse is a good example to start with. As the promoter of the law ending most penalties against homosexuals he has done useful service, but most of his bombs now fizzle dreadfully as a result of exposure in youth to more serious reading of the Viennese psychoanalysts than is becoming in a Welsh solicitor. It is not possible for Abse to explain incomes policies,

93

monetarism, the Falklands, devolution, or local government without bringing in the Oedipus complex or infant trauma. The leadership of the country by a woman has given him limitless scope for mother fixation. Abse is a joke wearing fairly thin. His stupendous, didactic conceit offers infallible diagnoses to a House fretting on the analyst's bench, and irritates now more than it amuses. He should however be given credit for being a sartorial dab of primary colour against the tailored melancholy of the generality. A wearer of atrocious checks and eloquent bow-ties, he favours a style of dress which middle-of-the-road commission agents would think overdone. No human act is without explanation in the subconscious and one comes to the tentative conclusion that the subject is attempting, without understanding the process, to draw attention to himself. It is, perhaps, a cry for help.

On the Conservative side we have Winston Churchill demonstrating that without much talent you are quite likely to fail. It is a pity, for Churchill is a friend of honourable causes and an enemy of totalitarianism. He also cashed in his political prospects by speaking out of turn on the negotiations which turned Rhodesia into Zimbabwe. As Mr Mugabe's North Korean-trained palace guard and Mashona *baaskap* supremacy establishes itself amid the debris, that doesn't look like long-term bad judgement. One speaks now of 'Peter Carrington's cleverness' with some irony. But it is Winston Churchill's misfortune that even when correct he cannot get himself taken seriously. As a speaker he is like one of those Englishmen abroad who try to be understood by shouting slowly in English. As a speaker he lacks every refinement. He is the sort of chap who uses phrases like 'groaning under the yoke of Soviet oppression'. He is an involuntary disinformation bureau suggesting that those most opposed to the Soviet regimes in Eastern Europe must necessarily be solemn hortatory fools.

He is the victim of many things, not least a preoccupation with his grandfather and a total lack of his grandfather's sense of humour. It would be cruel and less than accurate to say that he is much more his father's son. Unlike Randolph Churchill he is sober, unlike Randolph he has no towering hysterical temper. He is earnest and hard-working. He would actually make a better Junior Minister, given his devotion, than many now filling office. Alas, he has no weapon except indignation. And for a quite young man he has the solemn habits and formal style of an older generation of established politicians. But he does stick to his causes, he is a friend to Soviet dissidents, to the Poles, to the Ukrainians. There *is* merit there, in desperate need of refining and developing. But his confinement to heavy protest makes him a mirror image of some of the people sitting opposite—the heavy dragoons of anti-colonialism.

On these one could luxuriate. The House would be a gloomy

place for sketch writers without David Winnick, Stan Newens and Ioan Evans. There is no harm in any of them. Like Winston Churchill they have their good brave causes, fought vicariously, for Africans and South-East Asians, most of whom since those battles were fought and won seem to have come good and properly under a yoke of oppression.

Winnick, a much nicer fellow privately than publicly, has a squeaking passion which is moved to some very high tenor notes when, say, Ian Smith or General Thieu has been the subject. (It is a melancholy thought that the enemies of Winnick crumble while the enemies of Churchill get behind their water-cannon and remain in People's Democratic majesty.) He is slightly reminiscent of one of the dimmer *jeunes premiers* in a play by Arnold Wesker.

Stan Newens is inexpressibly nice. He could call for mass liquidation of the bourgeoisie and somehow make us see the charm of the idea. One can never get a full grasp of Lenin's maxim about the 'useful idiot' without watching Winnick and Newens. They are not Soviet-liners, nor the best judges of a hard and cynical world, they are innocents at large. The one nearly academic, the other nearly working class. Natural demonstration-fodder, they could walk down Oxford Street with a police escort, each holding the pole of a placard the way other people go jogging. Nuclear weapons, nuclear power stations, NATO, South Africa, Central America, Chile, Turkey, Polaris, Trident and, since they are nice boys, Poland. All are on the agenda. Protest has been to them what television is to the mentally underprivileged, something which fills up their lives and gives them something to do.

There are subtle distinctions though. Winnick has the temper and can break glass with fierce little outbursts against some 'vile, wicked, unspeakable fascist regime'. Newens, however indignant in principle, can never lose his gentleness. His denunciations are rolling, melancholy affairs; the malice, which abounds among the orthodox Left coterie of calcified men and quite indescribably awful women, is totally absent. He is the only person I have ever heard transform the sharp-edged accent of East London into a burr.

Ioan Evans by contrast is blessed with being Welsh. And as Jim Griffiths once put it in a by-election, 'Up 'yer you speak Yorkshire which is beautiful to the ear; Arthur [the candidate] speaks Cockney and that sounds very fine as well, but boys, I speak the language of heaven!' To listen much to Ioan Evans is to find the beginnings of sympathy with Roy Jenkins. One understands what he was trying to get away from. Broad-chested, dark-suited, Evans sits with the Hooligans for no definable reason. He is no Hooligan, Ioan, he is a windbag. There is a practice, detested by many Welshmen, of 'putting on the Shoni', playing the stage Welshman for charm and easy indignation. Some of the best, like Bevan, Griffiths and

Kinnock, have done it, so alas does Evans. The eloquence just comes like steam pressure in a well-run, old-fashioned boiler-room. If you ever wanted, for the purposes of some foreign exhibition, to demonstrate a working model of a Labour MP, you could do no better than to send out Evans, freightage. Everyone will want one. Well, nearly everyone.

There is a danger of suggesting that the Bomb Throwers among politicians are all idiots or fellow-travelling with idiocy. In fact, they include people who have more utility than half a dozen Ministers of State and more flavour than a frozen side of government. Enoch Powell happens to be being deployed elsewhere in this account, but he is of course the tutelary saint or treble-horned goblin of Bomb Throwing. He is also the leading Member of the House of Commons.

Sir Ronald Bell, who died before this work was even begun, was the object of thick-headed rage—'Death of a neo-Nazi' as *Labour Weekly* put it. In fact he was a lapidary and laconic hero of political nonconformity, a man with the talent to become Attorney-General who quite deliberately decided to be his own man, to speak out of turn, to reject a consensual view he thought naïve and wrong, and to reject preferment in the process. He disliked heavy immigration and opposed it without raising his voice. His argument was that small minorities are benevolent and well regarded and that large minorities become both the objects and subjects of conflict. He also took the view that since what are grimly called communities have been known to dislike each other, it is sublimely unintelligent to pass laws which require them under statute *not* to dislike each other. He also, to his great glory, had a huge contempt for statutory feminism, for the Equal Opportunities Commission and all its preposterous works. Being his own man, he had no obligation to follow any ticket, and so he voted for the abolition of the death penalty, the easing of divorce and the legalization of abortion. These are mere facts, tedious evidence to confuse a comfortable stereotyping which requires people to be 'left-wing' or 'right-wing'. Ronnie Bell was a quiet, grey haired, slightly built man who sat on the Tory Hooligans' bench but who opened his mouth only to say something sardonic out of the corner of it. He almost certainly gave most offence to the prim end of the Tory Party—those who rested their critique of the present balance of races upon things *they* had said in the past. He was liable to remind them that they had said that it would be monstrous racism to have *any* immigration controls before the first Tory restraints in the early sixties, leave alone Uncle Jim's fiancé-denying portcullis later in that decade. The topic, as he often said, was inseparable from humbug. And the great virtue of Ronald Bell was that he said out loud what conventional politicians later did.

Another outrage is Alan Clark, who adores to shock. Again, he has all the requirements for office. But his disinclination, unlike Sir Ronald's, is that of the cavalier who is having too much fun, rather than that of the heavily committed counter-idealist. Clark has been called a fascist, but only by himself. He is the only Tory I can think of who seems to take Clausewitz seriously. He is a sort of intellectual wild man who again cannot be placed in the spectrum. His contempt for conventional views leads him to a certain *tendresse* for the Soviet Union on the grounds that it has the only decently Machiavellian government in sight. He rather likes baddies if they have a touch of resolution. Unaffected by any sort of hypocrisy, he sees the world in terms of power politics. It may be a reaction against his father, Lord Clark, compère of the Civilization Show. But he is not a lightweight. He has knowledge in some depth on military matters. He is the master of the short, interjected, unanswerable question. His intellectual contempt for the pussy-cats of self-advancement would curdle type. His day-to-day involvement in the debates, statements and question sessions concerning the Falklands were particularly sharp and detailed. Of all the Bomb Throwers he would be the most formidable in office. He could take one of the Service jobs and scatter gold braid like rabbits in a cornfield. It won't be done but it would be wonderful to watch.

In a slightly different mould, Tony Marlow is someone who ought not indefinitely to stay outside. Also outrageous, he has shown the ability to floor the leader of the Opposition, admittedly not as demanding a task as it used to be. He has also given quite admirable hell to Mr Heath:

Heath: And we have of course a trade with our community partners which has increased every year since we joined.

Marlow: I am most grateful to the Honourable Gentleman for giving way but could he, er, say if the trade was favourable or in deficit?

He spends a lot of time in the chamber and functions, in a gentle sort of way, as a Tory Hooligan. Mr Heath, who detests giving way during a speech, partly out of self-importance, partly from deficiencies in riposte, on one occasion declined to take points half-a-dozen times and was subject to a gentle murmur of polite contradiction for great tracts of his trombone solo. Among the Tories this is considered bad form; and Marlow has probably been dismissed as impossible.

In fact, he is one of the best of the new intake with a good mind which can take on an argument and think rationally. He simply has a measure of good-natured exuberance which would not be noticed on the Labour benches. If he has a cause which is not good for his career—like strong sympathy with the Palestinians—he goes ahead and vents it. But if he were to make a New Year's resolution to become an orthodox politician, cutting out the sharp edges and working for promotion, he could get it. There are plenty of exasperated orthodox politicians who like him and would welcome him. 'The question is', said one of them sharply, 'does he want to *do* something or does he want to finish up like Nick Winterton?' It is a shrewd question which Tony Marlow will have to answer.

Winterton, although a devoted constituency MP, is fundamentally a failure. He is one of those younger older men, a patriotic rowdy, who weekly assassinates his own reputation by giving quotations to Mr Christopher Moncrieff of the Press Association for his weekly selection. This is made up of things painted in scarlet expressing the opinions of Buxton Spa majors and browsers in Collet's. If one was in the business of straight talks to young Members one would amend Mr Attlee's advice 'Specialize and keep out of the bar' by adding 'Never speak to Chris Moncrieff'. Many young lives have been blighted in that way. PA's recruiting sergeant wants a bit of sex and violence for the end of the week; to be used you must be wild and extravagant. Once established as a regular PA quote and the whips start drawing lines through your name. Winterton for one and Jill Knight for another have passed into the annals of political dereliction by such accommodation. While Mrs Knight takes it all with strong-minded cheerfulness, Winterton knows he has lost, has made a fool of himself and is barred not only from office but also from being taken seriously, which for the man who called De Lorean a crook is a pity.

Accordingly, there is a light of resentment in his eye, a snappishness and a tendency to get wilder. The same thing can happen to Aspirants who have miscalculated, like the atrocious Julian Critchley, who sought very dedicatedly without winning it, the lady's approval; and has accordingly been on general offer as freelance henchman to a sympathetic patron. In a newspaper article he wildly compared the supporters of Mrs Thatcher with those of Mussolini. Critchley's problem is that he started as an Aspirant but got a free transfer. He is thus obliged to go around posing unconvincingly as a High Tory. A petulant expression on a sea of jowl, he is rather like a character deleted from an early draft of a Simon Raven novel; small-time military, provincial press journalist, striving in a portly way to be raffish, Critchley has been passed over for a dozen good reasons (according to one story, when lobbied about the TSR2 in the mid-sixties, he turned out not to know what it was) and burns with animus for those who did the passing.

Critchley is untypical of Bomb Throwers by his disagreeableness. The Tory rebels are an altogether more amiable bunch than their Labour equivalents. The reason lies in a temperamental difference between the two Parties. Labour at the best of times is a violin taut and over-pitched. It is a protest Party. It attracts strong, fierce temperaments all round—Denis Healey and Hugh Gaitskell quite as much as Eric Heffer or Stan Thorne. If you want your politics stressful, you can have them that way in positions of responsibility and at all points of the Party compass. The threshold of excess is vastly higher. Accordingly to be enraged you have to work at it. Most of your colleagues are liable to say 'Go on, shock me.' And in fairness the effort is made, whether by Screaming Ron Brown or by 'Snarling Grandad', the less than altogether nice Mr Frank Haynes, who has the style and address of the delinquent element in a geriatric ward; or yet again by poor old Andrew Faulds, six characters in search of an actor. Most Tory wild men are easy going fellows whose wildness consists in the very fact of dissent itself. The Conservative Party suffers from an excess of tranquillity. It is double-booked with indistinguishable young men, usually called Tim, in dark suits, wanting more than they can ever bring themselves to say to become parliamentary private secretaries. Even a comprehensive buffoon like Michael Brotherton would, if transferred into Labour terms, be only a mildly eruptive back-bencher in perfectly good esteem. Nigel Spearing, on the other hand, of Newham South, whose Mussorgskyesque thunderings are considered solid back-bench work by his Labour colleagues, would be written off in a day within the context of the Conservative Party, as being in need of a darkened room and forcible restraint.

By contrast, Nicholas Budgen seems likely to remain in permanent internal opposition, since defiance of the whips, which is a cachet and proof of manhood across the floor, is proof in his Party that one 'lacks a certain indefinable quality' (which can instantly be defined as obedience). Such a judgement will be a loss to office but a benefit to the House of Commons's vitality. Of all those throwing bombs, Budgen causes most casualties. The heir of Enoch Powell in Wolverhampton South-West, he makes a very similar sort of trouble, not so much about race, an issue with which he is rather less fashed, than on the soundest of sound money policies and on Northern Ireland. On that issue he resigned office and proceeded to organize all the hell that he could call up for poor, dogged, laborious, goodwill-proclaiming, dead-wrong Jim Prior.

As an intervenor he is always menacingly polite and usually difficult to answer. Denis Healey for one, thumb-on-eyeball fighter that he is, has found himself rather behind schedule and needing to get on in a speech when the questions were coming from Budgen. It is not just that he is good on the economy, unlike most barristers in politics he seems to have learnt something from his profession about short, pointed and loaded questions. He can make a well-intentioned front-bench spokesman shift from foot to foot. He is not

intended by God to be a Minister of State, but neither would Mr
Moncrieff get a call for the machine-gunning of the TUC out of him.
He is a high-caste, slightly eccentric intelligence which supports
those things which the Government says it supports and wonders
aloud most civilly why perhaps they are not actually done.

At the point furthest removed from Nick Budgen is the young,
pure and earnest Stephen Dorrell, whose right to say what he
thinks must be defended to the death. Dorrell was elected in 1979 as
a very young man almost under protest. Much of what the Thatcher
Government stands for he disapproves of. He would be at home in a
Pym-Heseltine Administration voting ardently for inflation,
expansion of the public-sector payroll, wage controls, price
controls—the visible hand of enlightened directive government. He
is a pretty good illustration of the way in which the Tory Party in its
vacuum years was filled up with ideas derivative from the more
autocratic Fabians and remained Conservative only in the broad
sense of wanting to hang on to what it had got. It was becoming an
assimilated party, accepting the essential convictions of its
opponents, if 'conviction' is the right sort of word to use about such
people, but wanting them served in solution. Now the virtue of
young Dorrell is not that he holds such opinions but that he has
remained true to them. Like the older David Knox, one of the very
few men who actually would like Mr Heath back, he has sought no
compromise that I know of. A sort of serious-minded Brocklebank-
Fowler, he could with perfect propriety have joined the SDP. Wisely
restrained from falling over the edge of that particular cliff, he has
made no attempt to accommodate. The contrast with, say, William
Waldegrave, hired by Edward Heath as his intellect-slinger, who
has subsequently played a cool game of being nice to his old friends
and admiring Mrs Thatcher all the way to the Joint-Parliamentary
Under-Secretaryship for Education, is instructive. Waldegrave is of
course much cleverer as well as much smarter than Dorrell. But in
spite of a certain choirboy righteousness, Dorrell is faintly
admirable. Politics is not for plaster saints, probably politics is not in
the long term for Dorrell.

Let us now praise famous men. It is Hooligan time. My editor, Mr
William Deedes, contemplating some enormity committed by
Dennis Skinner, once said to me: 'And you're responsible. You built
up that oaf as a splendid fellow.' This, as I explained at the time, is
mistaken. My predecessor in the gallery for the *Daily Telegraph*,
Frank Johnson, took the view that Skinner, as a breaker of glass,
recurring expellee and world-class mitherer, who upset the stuffy
fellows who want to read Civil Service typescripts, was in essence a
good thing. The trouble with Skinner is that he has roughly three
times the news coverage of the next-best-covered politician—some
members of the cabinet excepted. Compared with him even the *able*

Junior Ministers live lives as reclusive as that of Simon Stylites. They
can pilot through substantial pieces of legislation, make 'radical
new departures' but they remain, until promoted to the cabinet,
sedulous, incorporeal beings. Dennis Skinner's lean flesh is real and
he hogs Question Time, which the more majestic souls despise
almost as much as they resent their failure to be reported. And the
annoying thing is that Skinner is a terrible speaker.

It is an odd personality compounded from dynastic socialist
fervour (he has brothers, not yet in the House, who are worse), a
feeling for the manual working class as a nation and the general
tone of a Borstal graduate. Precisely because he speaks badly—his
sentences are in traction—he has specialized as a beater-up of other
people's speeches. A steady offensive mutter accompanies another
man's declamation, like rain on a corrugated-iron roof. Nothing can
be done. It must be endured. And just occasionally there is a shaft of
golden lightning, like his celebrated demolition of the unlamented
Reginald Maudling.

The wretched *boule de suif* was making a perfectly valid point
about the unproductive nature of British car works, stressing the
fact that it took a German worker X hours less to make a car than his
brother at Longbridge.

Northern Voice: Oh aye and 'ow long would it take you ter mek
one, fats?

Total collapse of legislative assembly.

Skinner has particular hatreds. Maudling, whom we are now free to
say was corrupt, was naturally an object of loathing. For Killer
Skinner is nothing if not fanatically honest. The most scrupulous
MPs will take a lunch, even from a journalist; certain others,
protected by the rogue-befriending libel law, as Mr Maudling is not,
will take a great deal more: what are called consultancies, fees for
laying on a House of Commons committee room to impress the
clients of some public relations man, oh and one or two other
things. Skinner not only rejects the civilized and uncorrupting pork
chop; it is questionable if he does not regard a cup of tea and a
biscuit as a Faustian pact. He is a sort of Stafford Cripps in steel toe-
caps.

His other hatred is for the gentry or, more exactly, those who
affect the ways of the gentry. The cult of civilized living, from
burgundy to monogrammed shirts, makes him spit. Accordingly
the Social Democrats who, quite apart from having 'betrayed the
Party', tend toward the relishing of good things *en croûte* with a
bottle of very decent '73, reduce him to the condition of a sedentary
dervish. But the trouble with Dennis is excess, not only too far but
too often. A little Skinner goes a long way. There is a monotony to
him, a dentist's-drill quality, which always sets me in mind of some

ancient codger sitting in the park nattering into the middle distance. If it is safe to say so, for long tracts of time Dennis is something of a bore.

He is not, however, in the same class as Robert Cryer of Keighley who, as an articulate Skinner, is perhaps the single most oppressive presence in the chamber. He is not at all hateful but he has a youthful pomposity, a junior Polonius quality which one associates with borough councillors of the old school—'Further to that point, Mr Chairman. . . .' If Cryer had been a curate, Jeeves would have had to close the book on the great sermon handicap. Most sentences begin with 'But'. 'But, Mr Speaker, is it not the case that. . . ?' He is capable of raising difficulties for Governments, he does actually have good left-wing virtues of compassion and care, though he is not the monopolist of them you would think. The sight of him on his feet, index finger in the air, induces a powerful urge to slink away. While Skinner talks to himself, Cryer rises—on points of order, on SO9s, on interventions, and to make many many speeches of full length. He composes at Mahlerian length with the talent of Raff.

There is only one Liberal Bomb Thrower, Cyril Smith, and he lacks the essential good nature of Skinner and Cryer. With the most spurious reputation for affability in the House, second only to Mr Callaghan's, Smith plays the stage Northerner, like Skinner and Cryer. We are supposed to think Cyril shrewd (and since he offered comprehensive opposition to the Alliance and hoped in advance that the SDP would be strangled at birth, there may be something in that) but he is fundamentally misanthropic, one of those professionally plain-spoken men whose guile just occasionally shows. His outsiderism has little to do with principle, it is based on a streak of ill will towards the human race, much of which gets concentrated on his fellow Liberals.

While Smith manages to get one of those terrible phoney, plain blunt man reputations, like an over-acted character out of J. B. Priestley, Willie Hamilton can count on either derision or vilification in the press for his republicanism and hard words about the less useful members of the Royal Family. Yet he is basically a nice man, too often cantankerous, but as honest as can be and with all his faults up-front. There are two delusions about Hamilton—that he is a Scot and that he is a left-winger. Despite representing Fife Central and calling Princess Margaret a parasite, Willie Hamilton comes from Shiny Row, County Durham, and on most issues is on the moderate end of the Labour Party. He did in fact take the seat in 1950 from a Soviet tape-recording, Willy Gallagher. His trouble, that of most Bomb Throwers, is that he has never learnt the utility of understatement. There is an intelligent critique to be made of British attitudes to their royalty—the puffing done by the press, the orchestrated ecstasy, the better-than-Vestey tax deal, the thick-headed incivility of court officials. Moderately expressed, quietly reasoned and directed towards achieving, say, Scandinavian forms of monarchy, it would be a very useful counter-balance to auto-loyalty. If Willie Hamilton had been less seduced by the sort of quotation hunter who says 'Go on, bite their throat out', he might have troubled the Balmoral folk. As it is, Hamilton keeps on getting ever smaller bangs with the same bomb.

This will happen in time to Tam Dalyell if he is not careful. He starts off as a curiosity. There are not many thirty-first lairds and nineteenth baronets representing Scottish constituencies for Labour. Not many MPs give the impression of being eight feet tall and speak in a parody of the Eton accent which must give pleasure on the Hill. Nor do they denounce the Falklands expedition as 'stark lunacy'.

But what really makes Dalyell a Bomb Thrower is a stupendous arrogance or courage or stubbornness or all three. Where other men, asked to desist, would, with a longing lingering look behind, sadly desist, Sir Thomas goes on. An ancestor fought for the Romanov Tsars 330 years ago. Another was known to the always succint Covenanters as 'Bluidie Dalyell'. The term has been heard more recently. But the truth about Sir Tam is that if you happen to agree with him, then he is quite marvellous. Not only is it inconceivable that he will flinch back into the official party line, he will devote a vast genius for making trouble to the discomfiting and if possible annihilation of the authorities.

His family may have fought against the Covenanters but, temperamentally, he has all the rigidity and fixity of purpose of Peter Poundtext or any of the war-making Calvinist ministers in Scott's *Old Mortality*. He is a wonderful man to go into the jungle with. Nothing whatever frightens him. He was against the Falklands expedition and had only one intelligent ally in that unequal struggle, the sharp and to-be-watched-out-for George Foulkes. Most of the Labour front bench, while some of them longed for a disaster, went no farther than a drizzle of United Nations patter; and quite a few Labour members actually wanted the Task Force to win. Sir Thomas got up every day, to protest, to raise points of order, to denounce 'the entire lunatic operation', to tell the world about unproclaimed differences between ourselves and the Americans, and about the coming collapse of our trade with South American states. He lost, and only a naval disaster could have won for him. But it is entirely typical that he should have fought and fought head on. He is the antithesis of the creep. The contradictions of which he is made up have been personally selected. He is, for example, broadly 'moderate' in Labour Party terms, but for obscure reasons to do with a passionate hatred of

Pakistan he is able to live with the Soviet occupation of Afghanistan, an attitude otherwise confined to Screaming Ron Brown. His great moment came over Scottish devolution. That it was official Labour Party policy was a minor incentive. Sir Thomas was against it and spent months bullying and arguing. There is a nervous-breakdown-inducing quality about Dalyell every day on the day in full, Etonian, lip-curling voice. While George Cunningham got the rules changed for the 40 per cent requirement for the referendum, and Teddy Taylor turned the Conservatives, Tam just broke the Government's spirit. One would not be without him for worlds; a natural argufying rebel, not a stupid boor, not a failed creep working off resentment, but someone who is Out by taste and preference and thus free to fight only the battles he cares for.

Not all Bomb Throwers are admirable. Some have a stupidity unlit by any other quality. One thinks of Mr Winterton with his inability to be anything except furious in a predictable and repetitive way. Even so he has won the reputation of being the thinking man's Michael Brotherton, a stout, slow-minded soul in coloured shirts with white collars, whose contributions have all the nourishment of budgie seed. One thinks of Mr Geoffrey Dickens and turns sorrowing away. Near equivalents to one another, and altogether more admirable, are Sydney Bidwell, doomed for ever to be known to Conservatives as 'Good Old Syd' and Mr John Stokes, who by some administrative oversight is not Major Stokes.

They are among the best-loved Members of the House, Mr Stokes being the last of the old-time, king-and-country, military-moustache, prep-schoolmaster, values-of-1912, straight-bat and patriotic-loyalty men. Mr Bidwell is an equally old-fashioned, factory-gates-meeting, fraternal-greetings-bearing, what-about-the-workers, the-working-class-will-be-heard, old-time leftist, the last of another school. Syd Bidwell, despite his admiration for regrettable regimes of the far left, is, like John Stokes, so totally without malice that the old dears could with some felicity be asked jointly to make and second the Loyal Address. Stokes will be replaced by Tim, an inadequate marketing man on his second shave at 3.30. Bidwell will be replaced by a Camden Borough social worker believing in direct action.

But back to the criminal element. Dennis Skinner and his friends have been acutely embarrassed by the entry into the House of at least one Member who makes the entire bench of Hooligans look like civil servants. Screaming Ron Brown, who rushed at the Prime Minister in Scotland with outstretched arms until policemen grabbed him, is a young person of phosphorescent personality, and not, I would have thought, the House's most serene personality. The Labour Party's reaction is to pretend that he doesn't exist.

As for the official Hooligans they are left looking rather

aldermanic and middle-of-the-road, just as Eric Heffer (now dangerously close to becoming 'dear old Eric') was vehemently miffed a few years ago by the eruption into the House of cement-headed Eddie Loyden, a bawling, incoherent Liverpool dock orator, who could drown him out in any contest for the most vocal man on Merseyside. Eddie Loyden has now gone the way of Liverpool docks, but even he, with the subtlety of a crowbar, would seem modest and conciliatory in the company of a man whose wife said of his dash at the Prime Minister, 'I'd like to get my fingers round her throat.' Perhaps a seat will be found for Mrs Brown.

Slightly calmer but no nicer are Parliament's own Race problem—Reginald, and the only man who can vituperate in a low moan, the thin-haired, red-nosed, evil-tempered schoolmaster, Martin Flannery. This man wears chips on his shoulders like epaulettes. He was 'in the Party' and still favours its meccano prose. He is a surly, resentful and, more to the point, turgid fellow. Dr Johnson said the Giant's Causeway was worth seeing, not worth going to see. Flannery is worth staying away for.

Not so Dennis Canavan. The Member for West Stirlingshire really completes a trio with Skinner and Cryer and yet there is no difficulty in seeing him as a venerated senior Member of the House and, who knows, by some bold stroke, a member of the Speaker's panel. He is more interesting than Cryer and less weighed down with enmity than Skinner. He makes good-quality trouble, and has stirred Healey to controlled rage and Steel to a flaming pique. According to my learned competitor Mr Andrew Roth, he is 'anti: EEC, SNP, caning'. But the main quality is a good nature which keeps breaking through the conference-speech peroration—the shortest of his interventions tend to be perorations. Canavan is actually one of the good things at Westminster. Interestingly he is not a sociology graduate but a mathematician. He also has a church background—Roman Catholic, unusual for the Left. One is simply irritated that we are not getting the best of him. He is too anxious to lark about. One can understand the instinct not to join the queue of Aspirants. He is the one Hooligan who as a quieter, more conversational case-putter could transform himself into the sort of speaker one comes in to hear. He is like Tony Marlow on the Tory side, a considerable misapplied talent but much more extravagantly misapplied.

Some people are natural Out men but have, nevertheless, a serious purpose of their own. Sir John Biggs-Davison is a believer, a serious man, who uses the front bench below the gangway for guerrilla war on behalf of his convictions. Along with Winston Churchill, he lost shadow and prospective minor office by a vocal pessimism about Zimbabwe which was bad politics but good history. He is one of those systematic excoriators of the Foreign Office. Since the Foreign Office effectively determines policy in

Northern Ireland, it has enabled him to concentrate his interests. Sir John is one of those English Roman Catholics who find that their sympathy lies with the Ulster Protestants. He has usually been right on this topic and the various initiative-takers have been wrong. As a general rule the dreams of Hooligans are denied them. Northern Ireland could just be the exception. James Prior has so parodied the received wisdom by creating an Assembly which will have all the constitutional force of afternoon tea, that he may very well have done for himself. He is a much diminished man. And while the likes of Biggs-Davison and the other honorary Orangemen have not been subtle, they have been persistent. When the Ulster Assembly collapses Sir John and his friends will have the satisfaction of having told us that it would end in ashes and tears.

Julian Amery, who is the senior dissenter in this company and who works on the principle of finding out what the Foreign Office is up to and trying to stop it, is damned in his political style. The voice sounds like half a stone of best Victoria plums, the words are those common to a declamatory style best seen to advantage when Augustine Birrell was a name to conjure with; the gestures, though not extreme, have a little of the council chamber about them. He has been honest and consistent: he has offered loyal opposition within his own Party. He has often been right, but, by having the style of a toned-down Roy Jenkins, he disarms himself and gets his views bypassed because of the mannerisms.

His brother in antithesis is the great Eric Heffer. I know people who get very solemn about Heffer: 'Much more sinister than you think, that Heffer.' For better or worse I cannot see Eric in a sinister light. He is a heavy proletarian bibliophile once described by his old enemy, Mrs Braddock, as 'that thing Heffer'. He is to the new and rising sort of left-winger roughly what a respectable, old-fashioned, jemmy-and-sheet-of-mica burglar is to the sawn-off-shotgun trade. Like Amery he has a very emphatic manner, made up of a voice that carries, a strong, but not, thank God, Liverpudlian, accent and a way of sounding aggrieved.

But time in the House (class of '64) has had its effects. Not that he sticks out a little finger or carries responsibility to excess. But he has become an accomplished modulator. Someone like Dennis Canavan gets it wrong because he finds anything except fortissimo a sort of betrayal. Heffer has learnt a lot from James Callaghan. He can speak in a humorous non-partisan voice wondering sadly why those who disagree with him are so intemperate and unwise. Unlike most Bomb Throwers he has both held office and (in opposition) found his way back to the front bench.

Power does not shock him the way it does some rebels, for whom it has the standing of a crate of Bell's to the narrower sort of Methodist. In fact, to his personal disdain for Mr Benn he adds the scenario, not yet for screening, of 'Draft Eric'. This is not going to happen, but Heffer, who is better educated than Benn, if not in such exalted places, simply sees himself as better equipped to lead the Labour Party if it is going to be radically socialist, and if a leader is to come from the working class. As I say, it is not going to happen; but the next leader of the Party has posts of cabinet rank to bestow beyond the membership of the twelve-man executive. Heffer is in serious danger of being Right Honourabled, with only the Labour Party's popularity to protect him.

George Cunningham is in no such peril and George Cunningham belongs to the select handful of MPs one would set aside as being among the most valuable. He is the only SDP Bomb Thrower, apart from the lovable and stupendously indiscreet Neville Sandelson. Cunningham has none of that touch of silliness which affects so many Bomb Throwers. He is a difficult Scotchman who gets out of line if he thinks the line is wrong. His presence in the SDP represents negative rather than affirmative action. Huge rational contempt for the hysteria, the infantility and the rising authoritarianism in the Labour Party obliged him to go, and the mould-breakers offered the only hole available. He is a former Commonwealth Office civil servant and after that he worked in the Overseas Department of Transport House, as it used to be called.

Almost incapable of being impressed, he is sardonic and disillusioned. He had supposed things to be rational and has found them not to be. He was once very intense on African self-determination and a great excoriator of white settlers. I am guessing, but would suspect that that external motor which has powered quite a few people into a Party more militant than their general convictions, may have cooled. But if he goes out of politics he will be one free intelligence the less, and how many are there of those? In fact he will be a bigger loss than that. It sometimes happens that an able man who does not rebel for the devilment of it and who has very high abilities can pass through the parliamentary system almost unused while all kinds of office-holders chatter self-importantly on around him. It may be someone too serious, too lucid, too prickly. Brian Walden because exasperated with Parliament. John Mackintosh died of it, though both were hundreds of feet above its norm. George Cunningham has at least the satisfaction that he played a part in shooting down devolution, the last of the great absurdities of the seventies. That Parliament, the Parliament which managing autocrats so despise, should have stopped it strikes me as marvellous. The executive is intolerably powerful in Britain, whatever the liberal forms of the constitution. It is not a rubber-stamp or East European Parliament; but in their hearts civil servants, Ministers and whips do see it as a colonial assembly, a way of letting off steam, of rebelling, getting headlines

and letting the hair of Members be stroked by the sweet breeze of
newspaper and television publicity while legislation is duly
enacted.

Parliament does not begin to rebel enough. The whips are
intolerably strong, the bombs have badly circuited fuses and make
bangs without casualties. If the Bomb Throwers were really serious
they would combine much more. For the Outs, whether they are
patriotic military men, non-totalitarian socialists or just free
intelligences, have no more shared belief in the creation of, say, that
agency of corruption, the quango, in the Heath–Walker destruction
of good local government or a dozen other approved, wrong,
inevitable things than any other man who can think. I make no
apology for coming back in this book to devolution, it is the bright
example, the angelic instance of Parliament putting its collective
elbow in the eye of the executive and of the consensus.

Why not more? Why not a counter-consensus aimed at those
areas of polite corruption favoured by the governors? Philip
Holland, the industrious Member for Carlton, Nottinghamshire,
has spent years in making the quango a public shame, a mechanism
for channelling public money to holders of office in unions,
companies and local authorities. It is a sort of unit-trust version of
Maudlingism. The present Government does some deploring and
some cutting, but why has there not been a counter-consensus?
Why is not Dennis Skinner, who devoutly hates corruption, the
systematic ally of Holland? Even given that such things as quangos
are generally the creation of ministerial powers which lie
improperly outside Parliament, there is still hell to be raised,
sustained protest to be made. Why, even Mr Moncrieff could be
turned to useful account.

Why, to take another example, was there not a major
parliamentary bloodbath over that inexcusable piece of bribery (at
which even the Duke of Newcastle would have blanched), the
Humber Bridge, built from nowhere to nowhere to win a by-
election?

There are answers, and the equivalents of Sir Humphrey Appleby
(and his fellow spirits in the whips' office) take them for granted,
having created them. A major part of Ministerial power is out of
Parliament—in orders and directives which can only be shouted at.
Also there are government jobs, and always, it seems, more of
them. We have suffered under Wilson and Heath a sort of verbal
inflation in titles. Straightforward Ministers of a Function became in
a rush Secretaries of State for a Fancy Word. And as they became
greater men they needed more, higher-titled (and better-paid)
deputies. Education, to take a single example, had, in Mr Attlee's
day, a Minister and a Parliamentary Under-Secretary. Today that
Department of State, as we must call it, has a Secretary of State, a

Minister of State and two Parliamentary Under-Secretaries, and Education is by no means the worst offender. There seems to me no coherent reason why the Departments of Environment, Employment and Education at least should not revert to being simple Ministries, and why savage cuts among the underlings should not be instituted everywhere else. The Foreign Office, which survives as a Mogul empire beyond its time, would do well to have, simply, a Minister and two deputies.

But mouths are for putting sweets into. And with ninety government posts, all paid, as many opposition spokesmanships with the prospect of a paid job on election, and with around twenty-five PPSs on each side (even number two Ministers have taken to employing one of these), there are a lot of sweets around. In a House of 630 a figure of not less than 225 must be in some kind of post, however footling, for even a shadow number three has his dreams. In such a Parliament, it takes either inexperience, an indefinable quality of repellence, or actual disinclination *not* to become the holder of some position. It takes extreme courage to pull the emergency cord on the gravy train, as happened in the case of the Northern Ireland Assemblies Bill. Both Parties believe in incentives when it comes to keeping their troops in order; and there are prizes enough to go round.

There is one other problem for those who wish to run a counter-consensus. They are not as good as they should be in the mechanics of procedure. The two back-bench specialists, Michael English and Robin 'Hybridity' Hyslop, are respectively a larker-about and an eccentric. The great virtue of Cunningham has been a grasp of the correct procedures for pouring sugar in the petrol. Only a few of the able or of the deeply convinced go into what the Soviets call internal exile. It is not a promising career though a couple of clever men, one in each party, could turn the counter-consensus to account on a range of selected issues, making life hard for the party line, if not indeed impossible. But for the time being, most Members will seek high office. Perhaps we should turn away from the serious business of confounding absurd policies and see which of them is likely to get it.

7

Tipster's List:
Front Row, Fly Halves
and Hookers

Who's a pretty boy then? That is a question often earnestly asked by youngish men on the margin of office. The House of Commons has a good dozen former future Prime Ministers. One of the saddest things that a young politician can hear about himself is a twenty-five-year forecast of eventually reaching such eminence. In practice there will be a life peerage waiting for him, like a freshly dug grave, as he makes his way from Minister of State to non-executive director.

But we have to consider lesser things. Who is going to get into minor office with hopes of further and better particulars, and who, already within the Government, will be moving up or down. One of the reasons why very long-term prophecies are usually wrong is that they concentrate too heavily on ability. Now, with a high-octane degree, you can expect heavy advancement in the Civil Service, but if you make it as Prime Minister, you will finish up like Anthony Eden—a man promoted within his abilities but beyond his capacity.

Forget the premiership, then, and think not of who is *papabile* but of who might make it as cardinal or even monsignor. A good example of the heavily tipped, widely admired and thus perhaps doomed is the Minister of State of the FO, Douglas Hurd. 'Douglas is wonderful, Douglas must become Foreign Secretary,' said an excitable whip friend of mine. Douglas Hurd is indeed very intelligent. He is also, rather cheekily, the author of four political thrillers. One hears that his colleague Andrew Osmond wrote the lascivious bits and Hurd wrote the political scenes. Perhaps Andrew Osmond should enter the House to take Foreign Office questions.

For the one clear thing is that Hurd can be as clever as Immanuel Kant, but as a personality in the chamber he makes Sir Geoffrey Howe look like champagne. It is possible for the official reports about a man and one's eyewitness evidence to differ only so far. He seems to have a classic Tory defect—ministerial ability combined with slow strangulation in public debate. Hurd has refined tedium, polished and improved it. He is a quick mind moving in departmental chains, like a ministerial ghost making his way with subdued clankings across the course of debate. It may be that there is a lively, indiscreet, interesting personality there, but if so it has been bound, gagged and locked in a cupboard. It should thus be clear that Mr Hurd is certain to enter the cabinet.

Another nomination I would make for promotion is John Patten, subject only to his not being carried off by the ill fortune which has him representing an unsafe seat in which the Social Democrats could perform above par. Oxford is not called the home of lost causes for nothing. Otherwise Patten is nicely placed. He is a progressive sort of Tory, but not offensively so. He has shrewdly subdued a natural exuberance. Unlike the militant Wets he can be trusted not to spit on the carpet. Attaining office, he was sent to Northern Ireland—there is a price for everything. He maintains good and civil relations with the moist parts of the Party but has always been categorical about the need for Mrs Thatcher. In a junior sort of way he is doing something of a Willie Whitelaw. This is very sensible, and the shriller Wets have a lot to learn from that approach. To be the first of the class of '79 to make office, to do so ahead of many horses with shorter odds on their heads, and at 35, is the proper start of a professional politician. To have won, while in the service of Mr Prior, the esteem of Mr Powell (who described his praise for Patten's prose style as 'a case of the silver vase calling the cream jug bright') is what a left-wing educationalist would call 'over-achievement'. Yet it is an amiable, unconceited talent with humour and relaxation in it. One should be clever but not make a fetish of it. One should be ambitious but not self-devouringly so. Patten looks like a good case of high-powered normality and one to be watched out for.

Junior Ministers generally should be differentiated. There are three basic categories: those with the talent which may, if the tumblers fall into place, bring them into the cabinet; those who are solidly on top of the job they do and can expect to fill it, but nothing higher, for a long period of time; and there is ballast. This commodity is provided because junior appointments are the creations of the whips' wisdom. They are put there not for some vulgar reason connected with merit but because Alice's dictum about everyone having to have prizes has a great weight with those who think they they get better milk from contented cows.

Hurd and Patten are category A men. Good examples of category B would be Kenneth Baker and David Waddington. Waddington is a thoroughly nice man who came out of the whips' office a couple of years ago and is now joint-number two at the Home Office. He will not quite go to the top, but neither will anyone ever hand him their hat. He is one of those soothing Ministers with the gift of being reasonable. Baker, master of fibre optics and other high technology, is a grander fellow but in the same category.

It is perhaps unkind to expatiate on category C, which is actually rather long, so I will start with someone rich enough and bland enough not to be stricken into a melancholy. Mr Paul Channon, hereditary MP for Southend West, is 48 years old and after twenty-four years in the House is Junior Minister responsible for 'the Arts', a job which, under any Conservative Government decently conscientious about the corrupting absurdity of state patronage, would not exist. The Arts, as against books, music and pictures, constitute a racket; and it is wonderful that the spending of money raised in tax is nominally supervised by one of the few MPs who could pay the culture protection out of his own resources. Smooth-faced, smooth-minded, void of human interest, Channon is an improvement on Norman St John-Stevas, and, as a hole in the air, performs quite admirably.

There are other appointments which make very little sense in terms of merit. I was once in the chamber when a thin man with brushed-down black hair was muttering under his breath at the dispatch box. I asked a colleague who it was. 'No idea,' he said, 'Try the Badge Usher.' 'Er, who is speaking?' I asked one of these elder grenadiers who know all the faces. 'Well, who was it?' asked my friend when I returned. 'Adam Butler.' 'Ah, that's why I didn't know who it was.' But in fairness Mr Butler is one of those loyal sons of fathers who do their duty however unexcitingly. They are the victims both of obligation and diffidence, honourably soldiering on with tasks which seem not to excite them.

Much more tiresome are those who rise without needing to. Mrs Lynda Chalker, a sort of flavourless Dunwoody, speaks the party line like a rather hectoring British Railway announcement. There is no need for Mrs Chalker to be in politics. She has no family duty to discharge, no talent in need of fulfilment. She is what a Young Conservative becomes, the enaction of a political career in a vacuum of kitten-like activity, but no discernible inclination to say 'I like the idea' or 'I violently oppose it.' She is without a single redeeming doubt, only ever interested in politics, and yet she is profoundly unpolitical. She is doubtless a splendid Minister, being in no danger of being distracted by a stray opinion or idea from the narrowest definition of her function. I have defined her as ballast, but who knows? She may have irresistible defects.

Of those for whom promotion is recurringly predicted, close to the top stands the present number two at the DHSS, Kenneth Clarke. He has a lot of faults, towering self-regard and devotion to the EEC among them. Also he found himself at the broken-egg-and-picket end of the NHS dispute. Even so the forecasters have almost certainly got it right. Small and combative, like a Napoleonic periwinkle, Ken Clarke is untypical of the Conservative Party in his enjoyment of a fight, in his ability to argue a detailed, bellicose case and to function without a hint of apology. He is agreeably often without notes, finding it still possible to speak in this naked state. He is a Clausewitzian, preferring attack to defence. His civil servants are, understandably, not fond of him, having never before encountered a politician with such a cool, unMessianic certainty of being right. Slightly podgy and exophthalmic he is still in the final of any beauty contest. There is something optimal about Clarke, a combination of political animal, vigour, working intelligence, caution and aggression, all at roughly the right point. Only an 'E' for humility detracts from this glittering report. This side of being rubbed out by hospital ancillary workers he is going to get into the cabinet.

Not yet for the cabinet but certainly for promotion if there is any justice in the world is Geoffrey Pattie, now advanced to Minister of State at Defence. Nobody much enjoys being called Under-Secretary for Procurement, his last job, a rude name for quartermaster. It is the sort of job which involves rare appearances to speak, and then largely to say 'No, Sir.' Given the Ministry of Defence's sound Soviet disinclination to tell anybody anything, it is a job in which sparkling is strictly forbidden. Which is a pity, for Pattie can sparkle and has the sort of sardonic, low understanding of politics which brings joy to it. His colleague, Peter Blaker, is strictly category B (and B-minus at that) but is the sort of ex-Foreign Office breeze-block wall perfectly designed for M.o.D. communication with Parliament.

One figure, widely regarded as irresistible, has made some of us slightly sceptical about him; to wit, Malcolm Rifkind, once George Younger's deputy at Scotland, also proclaimed to be very clever. Being half Scottish and half Jewish, it is hard to see how he could be otherwise. And he has never looked back from a half-hour maiden speech delivered at the age of 28 without notes. But Rifkind is inordinately cautious, perhaps understandably alarmed by the catherine-wheel personality of his former colleague in Scottish matters, Nicholas Fairbairn, a politician who carried his own health warning and whose spangled abuse—'I will make a pact with the Honourable Gentleman. I will give him my learned opinion if he will withhold his ignorant one'—were treasured in the certain knowledge that it would all end in disaster. It did. As the law officer for Scotland grew more and more like an up-market warm-up session at Caesar's Palace, so did Rifkind grow more anxiously sound. He *is* clever and, honourably, a resigner (on the wrong issue) when in opposition. But, although there is humour there, one also detects worry which may be partly accounted for by his constituency. Mrs Thatcher can have a wonderful election and still lose seats in Scotland, which becomes more Labour and more economically residual with every year that passes and Edinburgh Pentlands has only a 1,200 majority. But for the protocol which obliges able Scots to fill Scots jobs first, he is precisely the sort of person who would take one of the English law officers' jobs admirably;* alternatively he is the sort of cautiously liberal but practical person who might flourish under Mr Whitelaw at the Home Office. He is going to do useful work, but he plays too safe for his own good.

The future of Dr Boyson fascinates more people than the Doctor. Superb on television, nervous and middling in the Commons, he is, as the world well knows, a Labour convert, a Lancastrian who twirls 'r's like a drum major. He is also a hater of comprehensive education and of everything which stands in the way of letters and numbers. He is also a hard man on economics, having earned his doctorate with a thesis on the Anti-Corn Law League. But he is also a certain social class of politician—working class. Ten years ago a working-class Tory in Parliament was a one-man Bantustan. Like poor Edward Brown, the Member for Bath in those days, he existed for display purposes only like a plaster-of-Paris cake in a confectioner's window. This is changing a little; Boyson, who has the essential reactionary sense of that part of the electorate without whom the Conservative Party would not exist, is a tentative symptom. Even so it is a monstrous comment on the fingerbowl conservatism which dominates most selection conferences that so few children of the working class come up, excepting those elaborately disguised and fully deracinated. Rhodes Boyson, to his credit, quite hates the gentry—and their simulators even more so. The relationship between him and Norman St John-Stevas, when they shadowed Education together, needed enough asbestos to put Turner and Newall back into profit.

Rhodes Boyson is a good thing, though if he had bullied the universities more instead of asking for cuts in spending and leaving them to make the wrong ones, he would have done far better. The idea that universities are fit to take decisions for themselves is a liberal fallacy. They have a wonderful sense of rhythm but they need constant supervision. Boyson is also Mrs Thatcher's sort of

---

*The most likely next Attorney General is Patrick Mayhew, a patent-leather model of sedulous aspiration.

person, unguilty, unashamed, not in retreat. He would give a great deal to get out of Education and become that very necessary thing— a great illiberal force at the Home Office. It will not happen while Mr Whitelaw is around for the good reason that Boyson has been about as discreet as TNT. He is also vulnerable to a kind of self-parody. Rhodes is thought outrageous so Rhodes must say something to shock. It may give satisfaction to make the right noses wrinkle, but office is best climbed by the south col of understatement. He is, though, a man of wide and unparochial sympathies, very much at home in America and dedicatedly philo-Semitic, finding perhaps among those whom Stalin and the Foreign Office traditionally regarded as rootless cosmopolitans, a republic of intellect and merit. A move for him to any position in the Foreign Office would give the public school men turning to Mecca there every morning a shock which it would be a joy to watch. Realistically, he may make some progress but only in his own Department. It will always be a pleasure to have him around. He has a simmering ego and a violence of conviction which, however impolitic, increases the vigour of politics.

Often mentioned, but for no good reason that I can think of, is Lord Cranborne. Now there is nothing whatever wrong with Lord Cranborne. No man can be in favour of the Cranmer Prayer Book, and out of sympathy with the departmental memorandum to God which has replaced it, and not be a goodish sort of egg. But if he has any parliamentary talent I haven't seen it. And one is exasperated by the squealing pleasure which so many younger Conservatives seem to find in the company of the accredited heir to a marquis. Lord Cranborne, while conscientiously performing his duties, brings out the worst in his colleagues. He is a nervous and rather clumsy speaker and so long as the House of Lords endures, his best hope must be its Leadership. He will go much further as Salisbury than as Cecil.

When tipping politicians in one's best Epsom style, the preoccupation is necessarily with the equivalent of 3-year-olds, at least when discussing those not yet in office. But there are others who have held a position and lost it and who yet look wasted with no job to do; and there are yet others above the age of bright aspiration who, on simple merit, should be in there. The absence from any post of Peter Hordern, who is a fund of useful information and whom one actually does go back into the gallery to listen to, is very odd. He is one of those instructive but not boring politicians who just know things in their natural details, with figures to prove it. He is an elder and more relaxed Tory answer to Frank Field. He would be very near the top of any list of notable omissions. The ability is there, so is the inclination (he is quite at ease with the Thatcherian state of affairs), but not the job. It is a mistake. In a rougher, less sympathetic mould is Ralph Howell, a sort of Boyson in a bunker. He also hits the statistics but tends to make cases against overmanning in the Health Service too coarsely direct for their essential truth to be appreciated. An ungentleman farmer from Norfolk, he has a highly developed bump of utility, but his political touch is one that makes him stroke hair with clenched fists. One can see why he is Out but could imagine him doing a better job than many who are In.

Peter Tapsell is missing presumably because he is not on the Prime Minister's wavelength, though his wetness is of a less than oceanic sort. Unlike Howell, he is extremely well wired and has suffered from overpraise. He is another of those victims of the future Prime Minister syndrome. He is, in fact, in the slightly embarrassing position of being too prominent for minor office and, despite having been one of the shadow Treasury team, without the experience to claim anything higher up. Anyone not wanting to hire him has an alibi. But it is another talent unused. And how much talent is there?

Of all the slightly older omissions the one which is truly incomprehensible is Terence Higgins. Edward Heath appointed some mediocre Ministers, but his Financial Secretary was not one of them. Membership of the Heath Treasury team is understandably not helpful in the eyes of those who took office in the wake of the great Heath inflation/statutory incomes policy/'Who governs the country?' episode. Except that it should be remembered that mere Ministers, including perhaps poor Anthony Barber, had very little say in that anti-democratic phase when Heath and Sir William Armstrong, a civil servant improperly employed, did their Stratford and Laud act. Membership of that Government did not necessarily signify full knowledge of what was being done, leave alone approval. Higgins is not a monetarist but, in his own phrase, 'an eclectic Dry', one who wants to get debt and spending down without too much preoccupation with the total of coin, notes and means of exchange in circulation.

Of all back-bench speakers, if the Star of the County Down is left out, Higgins is currently offering the most. In the manner of a certain kind of American dietitian, he speaks often and little. Looking like an amiable and scholarly hawk—long, lean and exact, a former athlete gone to read—he turns the Privy Councillor's precedence to account, with crisp little speeches on the economy which say 'That's fine; that could be chancy but it'll get by; the other is, I think, a mistake.' They are wholly rational and, as such, wholly civil. The criticism is constructive, the support invaluable. Contrast him with the slightly whingeing tone of some other members of the Heath Government. Self-justification does not begin to come into it, for he is blessedly unreminiscent. The remarks are addressed to the problems of here and now, and how, and one has with him the experience of learning, of hearing a case reasoned through from A to D without rhetorical tricks, while the whole thing remains interesting. Considering the ability of essentially futile people like Soames and Stevas to get into Mrs Thatcher's cabinet, giggling at her behind her hands the while, the omission of a first-rate man not involved with *camarillas* of her enemies, was a grave mistake.

Suddenly, and to the annoyance of right-thinking people, Iain Sproat, who belongs in no magic circle, has demonstrated that office can transform a man's image. Sproat has been immensely vigorous in the House. What he doesn't know he asks about. If a regulation is in existence, he asks what it is for, and, if for no useful purpose, how it can be got rid of. More than most people in this Government he behaves with the vigour of a young man, the practitioner of a creative disrespect. Having been passed over at Thatcher Government Mark 1 for the subordinate Scottish job he had hoped for, Thatcher Mark 3 brought the altogether more interesting Under-Secretaryship at Trade, and it has transformed him into someone in the A category, promotable and visibly going up. But if he has flowered in office, as a prominent Labour Member generously said, he would always have expected, anybody making office within the Tory Party on his merits must be heavily relieved.

Those who do the appointing, an ad hoc committee of Mrs Thatcher, the whips and older and wiser heads, are horribly often like the England cricket selectors. They have a fatal weakness for the Pringles, Markses and Goulds of this world. Fowler gets in by inspired oversight and Jesty never makes it. The team is captained by a professional but the writ of the Long Room runs everywhere. The balance of power between Mrs Thatcher and the Long Room will be interestingly tested if she wins the next election. For all the caution which made her capable of the unspeakable fact of getting the leadership, she should by that date be able to make rather more appointments close to her own convictions.

The test of such power will come over the admired and detested Teddy Taylor. He is her man, her class and her cast of mind but not her creature. He was shadow Secretary for Scotland and indeed he had reverted to that job from Trade only because of the pre-eminent importance of the devolution issue. But taking on the SNP occasioned his defeat in Glasgow in 1979.

To fall out of Parliament from the steps of Number Ten is like waking from dreams of concupiscence to find yourself in a monastery cell. He had many friends in the Conservative Party for whom this result was the one consolation of the election. Yet he leapt over the monastery wall by doing the necessary Johnsonian thing and taking the high road that leads to Southend. Yet now that he is back he has hardly operated like a man set on office for its own sake. His passion, and he is anxious not to be carried away with it, is modification of membership of the EEC. He would like to see associate trading status, something usually rejected in argument by the not very compelling statement that it would be unthinkable for a country of our importance. Teddy Taylor openly campaigns against the EEC in its present form and does so in formidable detail. It is hardly the magic carpet on which to float back into cabinet and the sincerity of his opposition is complete. Despite that opposition to devolution, he has a Scottish sense of what amalgamation of a weak unit into something bigger can do for people in that smaller, poorer country. He has a nightmarish view of Britain as the Scotland of Western Europe.

Even if it is bad career politics he will not let up and his main role in the House has been to ask and say things which on that subject 'are better not said, old boy'. He has for the time being excluded himself by dissent from one of the Thirty-Nine Articles. But that is not likely to be a permanent condition. If the Tory Party is to change, to become more populist in the proper sense of respecting the public instead of kissing its babies and ignoring its wishes, Taylor must be part of that change. He is in the House because of his abilities and his opinions. And any Party which does not use them is not the republic of merit which it ought to be.

He is also in one sense rather Old Right in that unlike most of the leading Dries he will get up and make a case for capital punishment based on the practical facts of violent crime. If one defines populism as a high sense of seeking to know what people want and to respond to that demand, rather than to eat the fruit of enlightenment and spit the pips at the People, Teddy Taylor is the ultimate populist. He makes a quiet case for stronger criminal penalties because he represented working- and lower-middle-class Glasgow long enough to know that the chief victims of crime are poorer people. He is not vengeful on the subject, merely rational.

Underestimating him as a working politician is a grave mistake. As recounted, he swung the shadow cabinet clean round about on devolution. When Teddy had finished, Mr Callaghan's safe little bureaucratic exercise, whose dangers would affect only the future, backfired and deservedly brought down the Labour Government. It was enraged Scottish Nationalists who on 28 March 1979 made up the vote of no confidence which thrust the Labour Government into an election with their Gothic folly in ruins.

One hard combative man is worth three dozen assorted safe angels.

Another gifted man whom one would like to see go into his first job, but who seems to have attracted the evil eye, is Ray Whitney. He has the advantage of being clever and the drawback (for Mrs Thatcher) of having been in the Foreign Office. (Labour noisemakers regard him as the obvious representative of the CIA, MI5 and the Chilean secret police.) Unlike most FO graduates he is a taker of hard lines, unlike them he is for corrosive rather than emollient politics. He has got out of line; although ambitious and very keen to fill office, he has managed to be his own man. Lean, slight, tense, he is also rather well informed. His tour of duty in China as a diplomat coincided with the 'Cultural Revolution' and the attempts to storm the British Embassy compound. It is a more vivid experience of life than is generally afforded by merchant banking. Whitney probably fears rejection too much, in consequence worries too much, gets into states of apprehension which are not really justified. He chanced to be one of the doubters over the Falklands expedition, but in a sensible way based on his experience of South America. He can be funny. He has the sharp intelligence of a former professional soldier, his real problem is that the slightly elderly ease of the Commons unsettles him. His desire to move up comes from wanting occupation. One can hear Ray Whitney's fingers drumming. Given the chance he will be very good.

Another corrosive politician, and another of the ghastly lower-middle-class people to whom I should like to see the door opened, is John Townend. He is liable, as is everyone who comes up by way of local government, to be dismissed by those who don't check their facts as 'worthy'. That stupid word is a hole in the road in the Tory Party for anyone who came the wrong way round. He also succeeds in infuriating Labour by a succinct, knowledgeable businessman's dislike of over-priced wages. He is a mortal enemy of the Wages Council, an agent of unemployment by making wages inelastic. But he has command of facts, plain speech, a good deal of courage and again he comes from the Players and not the Gentlemen's gate. He meets a payroll as a successful retail vintner with a string of shops in the North, and has met another one in local government. So far from being 'worthy', as Chairman of Humberside Council, he killed the Council closed shop stone dead on his first day in office. If Mrs Thatcher wanted someone with her own sort of background and set of values, she could not do better than use the Member for Bridlington.

A gentler figure, but one who has shown notable off-beat courage, is Peter Lloyd, the slightly splay-faced Member for Fareham. Lloyd is soft mannered and extremely likeable; not used there yet but a perfect face and manner for television. He doesn't make a great deal of noise, and is not a natural rebel, which made his resignation of a PPS job over Northern Ireland a bigger sacrifice than it was for knee-jerk guerrillas. And Lloyd belongs to that minority of the Conservative Party with strong ties to the human race. This is the quality which would make him a plus on television.

The haw-hawing Tory voice we know and wince from, the Saatchi-trained, high-gloss humanoid, is the usual television option, or, alternatively, the Uncle Tom taken from his amusing regional context. They are wonderfully good at making one detest the Tories. The nice thing about Peter Lloyd is that he speaks in a voice neither regional nor above us. He is entirely natural. If Mr Parkinson wanted to show us that the Party he compères has a normal fringe he could hardly do better than use Lloyd on the box before getting him into a job.

Not at all likeable, but already promoted, is David Mellor, the oil-based Member for Putney, who will be murmured for further advance by the Long Room. He is at least perfectly competent but he has the consuming egotism of a younger Pym and is as agreeable as a mouthful of Brylcreem.

We must give a little thought to sackings. If X is to go up, who is that Y to go down? Butler, Chalker and Channon are all eminently dispensable. Then there is Barney Heyhoe, nice enough but desperately uninteresting, and there is Neil Macfarlane amiably filling a post which should not exist, the 'Ministry for Sport'.

At the very top there will always be speculation against David Howell and Keith Joseph because they lack the carapace of political brass and because they have never done the promotional job on themselves which has made other, more modest talents shine so bright. I would bet against it. Mrs Thatcher is not notably hard in her private dealings; and she is a respecter of intelligence. Given a hit man to work beside them (and Sir Keith has a congenial windpipe-stamper in Dr Boyson) both ought to survive on merit. Among the ambitious, Heseltine has Defence—and always supposing he does not try to stage a coup, he will be kept arguing long and late with military lobbies, milder than himself but almost as relentless. But a good reason for promoting the Commissar for the Environment was to do justice to his excellent, toiling and exasperated deputy, Tom King.

Tom King is not the most devastating thing in the House but in his gingery good-natured way he is as likeable as he is generally thought to be good in his Department. Whether he will go further is problematic. Three years hard in the Environment seems likely. Then there is John Stanley, who, outside the cabinet, handles Housing. Stanley never seems quite to put his act together, and the cabinet is already loaded with competent men who cannot articulate, but he is a man for whom the knowing make predictions. Another departure unduly delayed is that of the Lord Chancellor—Hailsham, a calamitous old flimflammer. Genuinely he is a character, he does go blessedly long on humour, but that includes ill humour. He has simply gone on too long, stuck as he is with both his real duties as a law reformer and the brown desolation of the

House of Lords which he must chair. But for the constitutional requirement that the Lords should be represented in government so that those representatives can answer for it, there would be wonderful opportunities for retrenchment. I never sit in the Lords gallery and look down without recalling the words of Van Roon gazing upon Paris from a high point on Notre Dame: 'What a city to sack.'

And what Ministers to sack: the foolish, poetry-writing, Irish-loving Lord Gowrie, the null Lord Belstead and various amiable inconsiderable presences, but so long as the House of Lords performs a function more usefully done by a major revision committee of the Commons so will these men continue. When Hailsham does go he will affect the cabinet, since there are reputable silks in Ministerial jobs. There has always been a Geoffrey-for-the-Woolsack faction, not very notably made up of Geoffrey's friends. He has, in fact, showed such steadiness under fire at the Exchequer that it is hard to justify a translation to the elevated oblivion of the chief law office. Patrick Jenkin is another possibility; and, although this would leave the cabinet log jam as it was, there is a case for bringing in the best lawyer in sight from outside politics, as Churchill did with Simmonds in 1951. The best lawyer in sight is Sydney Templeman—Templeman LJ that is, oddly passed over for the Mastership of the Rolls. It is a long shot but it would be by far the best appointment.

Among those whose removal would be less a convenience than a positive pleasure is Sir George Young. It has never been clear what Sir George is doing in the Conservative Party. He is a compulsive meddler and regulator. He is one of those people who object to our taking our own decision on smoking, and wants to use the technique of the wayside sermon to recall us from such folly. This is the man who has brought in the statutory car seat-belt, something which should be our business not his. His manner is busy, his nose pointed, his spectacles rimless, his total effect awful. One gets from him a faint notion of what happens when a man intended for holy orders jumps pulpit and seeks asylum in politics.

Under Heseltine, since the DHSS managed to unload him, he has been involved in 'the positive response to Merseyside'. This is a piece of systematic futility, like trying to get water to flow uphill, namely the nagging of industry into providing jobs for the worst work-force in Western Europe. Bypassing the Lancashire and Yorkshire towns which have lost employment because of super-competition from South East Asia, feckless, villainous Liverpool, which proceeded, by way of the anti-economic traditions of its docks and the Speke motor works, to the riots of 1981, is to be rewarded, though having Young and Heseltine in charge is an idiosyncratic notion of reward.

A man in the progressive camp but of a totally different quality is Tony Newton. There is no ego there, no passion to instruct. There is a great deal of compassion but it is not worn on the sleeve. He has junior office and might be marked down as category B—excellent at that level and going no higher, but if Mrs Thatcher wanted to keep balance by bringing up the sort of person identified in philosophy with her opponents but so much nicer than them, she could not do better than to advance Newton. In his quiet way he would make the perfect Prior-substitute and there really is no longer a need for Prior to linger after the fiasco of his Irish Assembly. Kleinworts and the Lords are looming. It could be a painless severance; and a man who has been put in a false position could be taken out of it.

The other Prior-substitute or non-abrasive progressive whose promotion would please many people is Michael Alison. He is a senior Minister of State, is trusted and very much liked. Without lighting any fires on hilltops, he is quite good in the House—honest, mildly humorous, universally sound. If we were thinking of killing off Peter Walker, the Member for Barkston Ash in rural Yorkshire would be an admirable Minister of Agriculture.

Descending again to the level where one hopes ardently to become number three at something, *please, Prime Minister,* there is a category of the slightly flash who could go on being overlooked for some while without general conflagration. Gerry Neale (who could win back some of my esteem by calling himself Gerrard Neale) feels himself on the edge of great things and sits quivering in anticipation. Although he has proved a useful fixer—of a motion which gave the Government a shove in a desirable direction over union legislation—and although he has a commendable zest for the pure hell of politics (a politician's politician, if you like that sort of thing), he could be left to quiver a little longer. Also in the category marked flash and also fairly sound in outlook, but something of a livery man, is Christopher Murphy. One would not not give Murphy a job but one would not hurry about the giving, leaving him time to develop interests in other things as well as the preoccupying business of getting it.

A meritable man is David Trippier who has got out of line to be difficult on behalf of textile and carpet workers in the North-West, ready to side with Labour over the Multi-Fibre Agreement. That treaty, if you are an out-of-work weaver, is a good deal less amusingly arcane than it sounds, governing as it does high quotas of Taiwanese and Singapore goods permitted in. Theoretically everyone is a free trader except where his own are concerned. Trippier, not surprisingly, functions as a crypto-protectionist. No self-respecting Lancashire MP would do anything else. He is the sort of patient trouble-taker whom one does notice from the gallery despite the absence of any gaudy qualities. He might feel it wrong to take any office, given present differences, while he is doing what a constituency MP should do. But in the longer term he is a useful man to employ.

Not worth a second's consideration is Michael Mates, the overbearing and unpleasant ex-dragoon Colonel who advertises a friendly-towards-Dublin approach which, given the wetness of establishment attitudes towards the Irish and their Government, he thinks might get him on. It won't. Nothing will. Some creeps, like Hugh Dykes, are fundamentally quite nice, just a bit insecure. Nobody ever called Mates nice. Nor will there be any prospect for the lady now known as Elaine Kellett-Bowman, a voice like a rather butch CSM, a face marked with the cartography of discontent, and a mind hand-carved in bone.

Despite a conceit which could be entered for an international award, Douglas Hogg will inevitably attain office. He is not particularly dislikeable but signally immature, at 36 rather like a very clever schoolboy who has not yet realized the full and monumental unimportance of being the first boy to get the right answer out in class. He is also a lawyer and some would nastily like to set a quota on the number of lawyers in existence let alone office. The spectacles glint, the finger wags, the voice minces, if that is possible. But he did on one glorious occasion reduce Mr Ennals, a former Labour Health Minister to gibbering. He was reading out an independent study purporting to prove the absolute merit of policy A.

Ennals: (Quoting) 'We have taken the view that system A has very high value.' There, that should be clear. It comes from an independent report. I am amazed the Government has not seen fit to. . . .

Hogg: (Dancing up and down) Read on. Read on.

Ennals: Oh very well. It doesn't make any difference. 'But, good as it is, we prefer B.' Well (splutter), that's absolute nonsense. For that episode one would forgive Hogg a great deal. One does.

An unknown face is John Cope, who once said shyly, 'I'm one of those MPs who people didn't know had been elected.' But he is of course a whip, and whips these days go much further than they used to. And the comment on John Cope was: 'Now that's the right sort of whip, a chartered accountant instead of a drill corporal. He has all the numbers worked out and he doesn't shout at you.' People like Cope, unknown to the general public but liked by the people they have to organize, can emerge in a reshuffle as the name nobody thought of. Civility in a whip, as John Silkin proved, though he overdid it, brings its rewards.

Universally tipped is Christopher Patten who writes the Prime Minister's speeches before she mutilates them. He does this in the company of a non-Member—Alfred Sherman, proof of an ecumenism on Mrs Thatcher's part which would bring murmurs of hesitation from a clergyman favouring rock Eucharist. Chris Patten will get something when there is something, but ladies like to tease, and Patten, who has the real gift of phrase and verbal elegance, really ought to function rather more at the front of the shop. He actually is a parliamentary talent though not excessively on show.

The hair is frizzy, the manner academic, the person could quite well be a younger version of Sir Keith Joseph. The *Honourable* William Waldegrave, who is promoted by so many for cups, rosettes and great things at Epsom, is unlike Sir Keith, for whom he works and who has taken to him with solicitous respect for his abilities, in being a child of ambition. A very adaptive young man is Waldegrave. Nothing much in the House, rather flat and routine in his handling of argument, but he has not only executed a graceful glissade from under Mr Heath's wing to a useful position under Sir Keith's, he has come to terms with the fact of the Thatcher regime while not being of it by conviction. He is an aristocrat and clever, a rare enough conjunction of qualifications to be one of those people about whom hopeful things are murmured. More to the point, for one so painted in white and gold, he could be mistaken for a politician. Sir Keith thinks the world of him because to that intelligence what communicates is intelligence itself. He will get on though, for he has talents of a less refined sort, like an unequivocal intention to get on.

A name not mentioned too much because he has disappeared into the whips' office, which is a grave with prospects, is Archie Hamilton. Hamilton combines economic views of a South Sudanese kind with the still useful Eton and Guards bit. His position in that whips' office promises something on graduation. He is South-Eastern whip, which means that in practice he has to deal with a useful hunk of his party. And, being one of the nicer men of politics, he is not likely to lose by that acquaintance. Something else, he is a member not only of the Hamilton family, who are strong-minded Scottish barons, but also one of the Ricardos, which is good genetics. There is a peculiar mixture there of good nature and conviction, relaxed manner and serious intentions, the old style and the new substance. He is an excellent equity with strong upside potential.

Highly recommended though not much in evidence, are some of the PPSs, notably Ian Stewart, who did for Sir Geoffrey, until his recent move up and about whom expressions of Owenesque admiration—like 'immensely able'—are used by people who do not throw such expressions about.

There is also Sir Keith Joseph's PPS, the villainous-looking Kenneth Warren, who has a background in doing things— aeronautical engineering to be precise—and whose sense of the comedy of events would make him a relaxing presence at the dispatch box. Either in a post at Industry or in one of the Service jobs, Warren, who has abilities and knowledge beyond his humour and good nature, would be good. It would also be satisfactory in a House containing too many people who have been professional politicians since they left university to see responsibility descend upon a man who knows one end of a ball-bearing from the other. He is another of those rough, uncourtly fellows of whom the Parliamentary Conservative Party has a blood deficiency.

Another PPS of course is *the* PPS, Mrs Thatcher's very own Ian Gow. But Gow is probably more *in media re* than if he were a full cabinet Minister, let alone a newly appointed Parliamentary Under-Secretary. He is a cardinal in the Curia; whether it would be an advantage to go out and become Archbishop of Cagliari is doubtful. But he is a nice man, a very influential one and somebody who smiles all the time with a mouth otherwise kept firmly shut. He has probably got the job he is best at.

I have mentioned the recently upshuffled Ginger Tom King. If politics split between cheerful men and worried men with Norman Fowler and David Howell leading the latter group, King belongs firmly in the first category. He has done a great deal of Departmental work, and, despite the impression of bias in the red-headed league, is a contrast to his late boss. Where Heseltine is impatient and given to crusading, King has a satirical bent not sufficiently indulged. On occasion he makes outstandingly dull speeches because he feels called upon to do so. But there is a light touch there. If it were employed more he would impress the public and the House as he already impresses backstage by his labours. The massacre of Denis Howell, the Robespierre of the municipalities, the sea-green platitudinous, was enjoyed by all who saw it. King's promotion was beyond question. How far he registers as a public personality may turn upon how far he relaxes the heavy responsibility bit and uses adversarial talents which are the more effective for their lightness. Geniality is not actually a defect in a hard-working Minister.

Discussion of Cecil Parkinson has been left to this chapter rather than to the account of the front bench for reasons of protocol. As Chairman of the Conservative Party he answers to no departmental brief. For a long period in the House he did not speak because he is another of these sinister whips who come up from behind like Victorian footpads when nobody is looking. His ministerial post was one which put him on the jet-lag circuit, as a drummer for exports, and I would hate to be part of a Bolivian Ministry which declined to buy something Cecil was selling.

He is big already, but he is going to be very big. He gives the impression of having studied videos of David Steel and to have been perfecting the *douce*, modulated, fair-minded insincerity of that young master. The television performances are very good and if he is wise he will cast himself as his party's front man. There is no ineffectual splutter, no defensive self-justification. He argues as if no reasonable man could possibly disagree with him, and he is invariably soft spoken.

For my money, Parkinson, who forms an old alliance with Tebbit, for they have known each other for more than thirty years, is a future Chancellor. His promotion to the cabinet was missed by almost everyone, yet no one should have missed it. He is at the spear point of the new element in Conservative politics. He has come through two of the three master schools (Trade and the whips' office—the Treasury is the other). He belongs to *this* leadership which needs its men in the places that matter (watch for the day when Mrs Thatcher promotes her present compromise Whitelaw nominee as Chief Whip, Michael Jopling, and hires her own man).

The Chairmanship and the Chief Whip are crucial to control. Parkinson will stay where he is for some time, moving only to a job of the highest importance. If the commentators missed him the first time so much the worse for the commentators. There is no excuse for missing him a second time. Notoriously fit and looking ten years younger than his age, he is also a rather hard man. Soft-spoken politicians usually are. Although he is excellent company and entertaining, he has aimed long and high. For my money he is on target to become ultimately number three or number two. It is a cool, measured, authoritative talent. Any idea that he is some sort of lightweight place man can be left to the people who couldn't see him coming in last time.

One could run through a longish list of category B men, like the funeral-suited Kenneth Baker, who makes his way plashy-footed through the fen of advanced technology, the improbable heir of early Wedgwood Benn at MinTech, who will probably remain just outside the cabinet but with real and substantial work to do. Mr Baker and those like him could be referred to H. G. Wells's bloodshot and grim-battling Morlocks and their glad, light, feckless neighbours, the Eloi.

It is inconceivable that there are not children of both ladies who have been omitted and whose writs may be added to those of the people who have not. But as *The Times* once severely said to Mr Selwyn Lloyd, 'Enough is enough.' They can rest contented with the thought that, with only a tiny break, Mr Lloyd continued in the highest office—Foreign Secretary, Leader of the House and Speaker—almost to the end of his life.

Necessarily this chapter is preoccupied with the Conservatives as the Government of the day and as the party most likely to win the next election. But a brief intermezzo of comment on the Opposition is also appropriate. Labour has every problem imaginable except lack of talent; until, that is, the day after Conference goes beyond conferring power of deselection on Members and takes from its representatives in Parliament the choice of their shadow cabinet. Its talent will also be diminished more gradually by not winning, and not looking like winning, elections.

The party can do one of two things, poised as it is in the foothills of schizophrenia. There is an outside chance of remission, of escape from the manic impulse which ends in broken mirrors and heavy sedation. This is the Teddy Taylor option, shrewdly set out by the Conservative MP for Southend East. It turns upon the unacknowledged popularity of a soft line on defence, especially nuclear defence, upon a stand intelligently but not rashly critical of the EEC, pulling towards associate trading status; and, above all, it turns upon Peter Shore.

Now Shore's virtues have been rehearsed but the point has to be made that Michael Foot is not going to win an election, not now, not ever. Hattersley for some obscure reason is thought of as untrustworthy, Silkin is not in the running, nor quite is Kinnock. A Shore leadership would still probably not bring Labour to power, but it would give some of the young and able men a reason for staying and something to hope for. To speak plain, he might haul the Party far enough back to give the younger men a career structure.

Capable of good things are the smooth Geoffrey Robinson, the rough Jeffrey Rooker, the obscurely but obdurately rising John Evans, Mr Foot's PPS who always suggests a pitman's whippet, the soft-centred, soft-outsided ex-President of the Oxford University Conservative Association, Phillip Whitehead, and the melancholic ironist and cool first-rater, Donald Dewar. These and a great many more wait under greater trepidation than the Tories. For it is not clear whether the word 'left' is destined to be an adjective or a past participle.

Clearly the cheerful 'I got a horse' job, which can be done with the Tories, is inappropriate for those in service under the present leadership of Foot and Boot. I can only observe a few talents and give some credit without presuming to guess what chance they will have of being used. Dr Gavin Strang instances the way in which a general violence of manner appropriate to Wishart and Knox appears compulsory to any rising Labour man. There are exceptions like the civil and persuasive Peter Archer whom a sensible Labour Government has decided to use for something better than a law officer. The relief of a non-grinding debater well this side of atrocity is noted and appreciated. Gavin Strang, by contrast, although part of the political mainstream, is fundamentally less tolerant and good natured than an accredited hooligan like Dennis Canavan. It will save him from de-selection but it is a terrible strain on the rest of us, and sound points have to be taken between snarls.

If he could be bothered, if, that is, he were a wholly political animal and if the Labour Party were a happier body, Dr Mark Hughes of Durham City would be worth following. He is gentle, subtle and capable of being funny in an old-fashioned, educated, literate sort of way. He acts as deputy to Norman Buchan at Agriculture, but the impression is of a man fully apprised of the encircling gloom but with no expectations of the kindly light turning up. Buchan, while we are in positive-NCA country, is a nice man, an old-fashioned left-winger with a clever wife who deserved to get into Parliament herself. He faces Peter Walker thus bringing the unvarnished and the lacquered into conjunction, but he has damped down his fire. The Norman Buchan of twenty years ago would have had Walker by the lapels. Now, like Michael Foot, though less disastrously, he has lost much of his dynamic.

Another shadow Minister, John Smith, suffers only from the obscurity which his name imparts, but has a great deal of insider following. He is measured and deliberate, making those concessions from sense to nonsense which the current state of the Party requires, but is still the sort of man who would be pushed forward in a hurry by any Labour Government to persuade the City of London that the expropriation of the expropriators is not in prospect, and that invisible earnings are deeply appreciated. Given a certain flexibility of mind in both men, one can even see Smith as Benn's Chancellor. Certainly if orthodox Labour have the office to bestow he will get it. And a Shore victory in Opposition will presumably put him into the shadow Chancellery. He is one of those utilitarian men who do not loom as strictly political stars but who get their fill of office, Marthas perhaps but high-class, $100-a-night Marthas.

The shadow Scottish Secretary, Bruce Millan, is a toiler, a man with the flair of a sandbag, snappy, irritable and petulant, having just that degree of sullen sufficiency which the post demands. He has never been in any other Ministry or shadowed any other. Since 1966 he has functioned as Under-Secretary, Minister of State, Secretary of State or the appropriate shadowship. He has been inside longer than the Krays. One takes back criticism of his petulance. After seventeen years of Scotland without the option, most of us, including the Scots, would be ready for a plain van and restraint.

Mention has been made of Jeffrey Rooker. He speaks on Social Services with effect and will go a great deal further. There was a time when he was seen entirely as a wild man. A sullen and ferocious manner persuaded many Tories that they had a ranting street politician among them. Since then he has done a great deal of work, mastered detail minutely and tempered his natural exuberant urge to stamp on people's hands to a steady, controlled antagonism. He is a very serious, extremely intelligent man, not playing at anything. It is entirely realistic to think of him as cabinet material. The leather jacket has been discarded, the 'You wanna make anything of it, step outside' style of debate put into unreliable refrigeration. Plain grasp and competence are the qualities one notices today. There is still a strong simmering prejudice. He hasn't been brought into the self-sustaining fraternity of the Commons club. In a desirable way abrasiveness remains, but not stupid rage and rant. Just a little cooler and he will be unbeatable.

It would be dangerous to be dogmatic about George Robertson to whom an earlier allusion has been made. He has the courage, at a time when quite middling Labour men scurry to CND, flatly to oppose it. George Robertson, who has an intelligent man's obdurateness, remains a believer in the continuation of nuclear defence against the prospect of nuclear attack and is a supporter of the Atlantic Alliance—an extremist in fact. He is not one of those inheritors of an old orthodoxy who simply trundle on with it. He has done his own thinking and written compelling papers on the subject. Now Robertson is precisely the sort of free spirit which the SDP needs like it needs blood. Chance, temperament and geography have kept him away as it has the admirable Donald Dewar. They are not the SDP's sort of people. You need, like poor Wrigglesworth, who plays the piano for Roy Jenkins, to check your soul in at the door for that. They are also Scots—and despite the close-run thing in Tory Hillhead, Scotland will not be SDP territory ever. It is cemented into Labour like someone in Chicago's East River. A right-wing Scottish Labour MP is stuck. He can either conform and lose his quality or be his own man and trust in the Almighty. George Robertson and Donald Dewar, one plump and brave, the other angular and funny, both immensely likeable, are too good to lose. Although they advance in the current twilight of uncertainty, their main effect is to cast your mind back to a day when Michael Foot, with all his virtues, was not the standard-bearer of moderation. For a short term they will flourish as factions are balanced, but I would regretfully put no money on their long survival.

Two other pluses for Labour who have acquired publicity since they entered the NEC are Betty Boothroyd and John Golding. Miss Boothroyd, who speaks with both candour and the semblance of candour, is set fair to become the Shirley Williams replacement. She has brains, she has reasonableness; and the job which Mrs Williams used to do as a bride of Dracula, sweet-fronting for the regrettable things in the engine room, Miss Boothroyd will do better. She has spent a long time getting into the House, not surprisingly given her

mild views. But she will move now. She is crisper than Mrs Williams
and has, literally, professional command of TV. How often does
either party get the allegiance of a Tiller Girl with brains? The soft
sell of Labour is coming and she will be an indispensable part of it.
One reverts unapologetically to TV where Parliament spills into the
living-room. The Tories would do well to bank on seeing Miss
Boothroyd up front, convincing, candid, very likeable, offering a
version of the Labour Party which is hardly known in 80 per cent of
the constituencies. She is an asset and will be used as one.

The other new personality, not at all intended for screening, is
John Golding. He is the Bill Rodgers of his generation, the
committee man of the residual Right. He has used the temporary
blessing of union support on the NEC with a ruthlessness which
worries his Soft Left allies. The policy committees have been swept
clean of the people who dominated them for a decade and more.
This is considered 'excessive', 'Stalinist', 'too hard'.

He has injured Labour's unity; since 'unity' is a concrete life-raft
which convinces the voter of a suicidal determination to conciliate
the people he isn't going to vote for, Mr Golding acts very shrewdly.
He would argue that a fight engaged upon and won will give the
electorate renewed belief in an authentic Labour Party it can blow
paper Xs to. It is probably a forlorn undertaking, but nobody ever
accused Golding (three votes behind Benn in the shadow cabinet
election of 1982) of not fighting. He shows signs in his arrival, of
being Blücher, but where is Wellington?

On his way out and ready to make a space for someone else is Roy
Mason. He has done his duty and lives now in the perpetual
company of anxious armed policemen. Despite the De Lorean
blunder, he was the best Minister Ulster had—matter of fact,
illusionless, deluded into no 'initiatives', fumbling with no
'dimensions' but turning to the Scotch-Irish and bomb-Irish and
saying in effect 'Look, I will give you certainty which is the next best
thing to the serenity which you will never have. My Ministry will
give you administration; the police and the Army will do all they can
to provide security, and we will have a period without tricks,
expectations or blueprints.'

That period of office saw a steady decline in IRA action. It was
straightforward and not tailored either to vanity or calamitous good
intentions in the Minister. Sense in a Minister has a way of
attracting no glory. It gives fools nothing to write about. So Mason
did not come back as the major figure he should have been, but as a
tired, less ambitious and exasperated man. He detests the drift
leftwards, has always been a sincere European and finds himself in
a Party making insincere anti-European noises. On top of which in
his constituency of Barnsley is housed the headquarters of the
slightly unreal Arthur Scargill and his semi-professional street

theatre group. It is enough to make a rational man turn away in despair. Although he stands reselected, Mason will not be in Parliament much longer. He will join the quality drain of men who turn away from the Labour Party without immediately resigning from it in comprehensive despair, in order to do something grown up.

This fundamentally is Labour's problem. It attracts talent, employs talent and eventually talent despairs of it. It is essentially futile to speculate beyond the broad outlines given of who will be In, who Out. Not because Labour is ill placed to win an election, nor because its victorious candidate in irreducible Gower returned the lowest share of the vote since 1931. These are roundabout matters and do not affect the avidity of politicians to get to the front of the queue for better times.

Labour is changing out of recognition. Yesterday's radicals are today's temperate men and the change is only a little in *them*, a vast amount more in the specific policies of the Party. If the Social Democrats were not the squabbling clique they are, if they had drawn the working-class Right of the PLP with them, they could have creamed Labour. As it is, Labour will be Peter Shore's empty inheritance, not fit for office, not likely to get it and waiting for the next division, the next nerve-jangling row. We talked of laagers. They exist and will keep something going. But we might have been on a better metaphor to speak of sandbars. They, above all jolly speculation, seem to be Labour's real destiny.

8

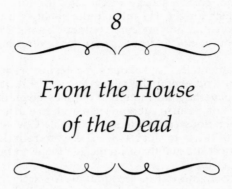

From the House of the Dead

How bad it feels to have fallen depends upon how far up you were and how much higher you had planned to climb. It also turns upon whether you jumped or were pushed. Politicians who have taken themselves seriously are the ones to taste the black bread of exile most sourly upon their tongues.

The Outs, like the Jacobins, rather favour the Mountain, the back and second back rows below the gangway. Mr Heath has his statutory ex-Prime Minister's seat, front below the gangway, where Churchill sat from 1955 to 1964; and God help the low coster who usurps it. When it comes to baleful glares, Gorgon Medusa is strictly a Sunday artist by comparison with the Member for Bexley, Sidcup.

We can come back to Mr Heath. There is no need to hurry. The back benches are full of people who used to sit on front benches. They can't all be ex-Prime Ministers. Some of them are ex-Parliamentary Under-Secretaries or ex-Ministers of State. Again, they react according to temperament. Sir Anthony Grant, the jolly stockbroker who was a busy Junior Minister in the Heath Government, seems rather to enjoy a fling as one of the bad characters on the Hooligans' bench. He seems to have no notion of the natural grandeur of a former Junior Minister.

That will never be charged against Eldon Griffiths. Mr Griffiths first came to the Commons from a long spell in America where he had been *Newsweek*'s political columnist, which is a first-rate job. On any estimate of the political market he should have got above 500: a rich marriage, overseas provenance, blind devotion to the EEC, a heavy sententiousness of the kind which politicians tolerate more readily than the scoffers in the gallery, and working-class origins (but beautifully glazed over by a sort of offshore American accent). He became Minister for Sport.

Now he is on the back benches. One has only to listen to Griffiths to know why he fell. He is self-important, and, to an impossible degree, he is mannered. Perhaps because he is cursed with good looks of the kind which make him look like a politician in a film, he rapidly became all bronzed profile and index finger. A Griffiths speech, even if it has good points, always contains self-parody. It gets up and says, 'This is something important, said by somebody important, so it behoves you to listen' (and he would say 'behoves'). There is in him a cocktail of turgid Victorian grandiosity and the banality of mind which accompanies a well-planned career. He is a slicker but not a very good slicker, an under-capitalized Peter Walker. Poor Mr Griffiths saw himself as an indispensable member of the Foreign Office team, having briefly been 'Spokesman on Europe' in the last (Opposition) days of Edward. One is sorry about that and about his disappointment, but really the FO is quite bad enough as it is.

The Mountain to which resigning Ministers retreat is associated with varying degrees of querulous resentment—a sort of integrated Doorn. But how politicians actually behave up there depends upon their own self-respect and working relations with the human race. It is still possible for a sensible man to be influential from those benches if the people up front think they are listening either to a reasoned private conviction or to a genuine representative of a back-bench opinion. Few do this better than Maurice Macmillan. He had a rough time as a Minister. The sons of famous fathers rarely have much happiness, but Mr Macmillan is a nicer man than his father. Yet Harold Macmillan could, and at 88 still can, slay an audience. Maurice is heavy and conscientious, and applied himself with fairness and diligence but no luck to the Employment portfolio in the melancholy, marching winter of 1972–3.

Like so many Conservative Ministers, he was tongue-tied and official, oppressed by his brief, and unable to carry argument forcefully to an Opposition which in its destructive irresponsibility deserved scathing attack, but which in that Parliament always had the emotional and moral upper hand. The capacity of the Labour Party for moral bullying is never sufficiently remarked.

Yet Mr Heath's Ministers took their note from him. To serve in the Government of a man half persuaded that the other side was right, in essentials if not in methods, was deeply demoralizing. Ironically, even though Maurice Macmillan does not often come the Privy Councillor, he made the best elder statesman's speech in years at the height of the Falklands crisis. It will be recalled that this military triumph had a number of kinks in it, notably marked in the Commons by a speech from Mr Pym which opaquely indicated that

HM Government was toying with a stand-off, blurring into a sell-out. It was received on the Tory benches like winter. And, as a Labour colleague remarked to me in the gallery, 'That is the Tories for you, chickening out.' The deep in-built conviction that 'the Losing Machine', as the Foreign Office is unaffectionately known, had brought off another coup, brought from Mr Macmillan a crisp, lucid, interrogative speech—which, within the requirements of civility, told the Foreign Office to get a better view of events from the top of a tree. It was beautifully done, and, precisely because the speaker was not in the habit of parading his opposition, expressed the feelings of the infantry with the force that comes from disinterest.

This is the beauty of British adversarial politics. Convention requires wide acceptance of a broad leadership line, but skilful internal opposition can communicate what will not be put up with. The Tory establishment had seemed for a while, independently of Mrs Thatcher, to lose sight of its own supporters and to head towards bathetic climb-down. Mr Macmillan's Very pistol came in extremely useful.

It is possible, of course, to belong to the House of the Dead even while holding office of some sort. Nicholas Scott, mentioned above, is a full Minister of State in Northern Ireland, but it is a wholly posthumous appointment. The soft end of the media still has a kind word for him, anxious as it is for 'civilized Conservatives' —spenders of money, welcomers of even more immigrants, improvers of our low lives. Scott's worst enemy would not call him an ascetic. He has the essential qualifications of an early sixteenth-century Pope. Fat, hedonistic, and known to the Divorce Courts, his face a harvest of broken capillaries, he is a standing reproach to Sir George Young and Mr Cyril Townsend. It is hard to recall that only a few years back he was one of those about whom the curse—future Prime Minister—was murmured. It is even harder to grasp, listening to his public school accent, that he is the son of a policeman and that he went to school in Clapham; even harder, looking at this Falstaff, to realize that he is not yet 50 years old.

Scott is in a job because James Prior wanted someone of like views and congenial nature to make his stay in the Congo tolerable. In terms of the Roman Empire, the post in Northern Ireland is the equivalent of being made sub-praetor for Eastern Thrace. Poor Scott is a willing victim of the social ladder aspect of the Conservative Party. He has devoted a career to affecting the style of a different social class, and learnt very early to reject honourable and reputable origins and to work hard at imitating the worst and most worthless section of the gentry, getting on to the drawl-and-champagne circuit like some snubbed minor character of Thackeray. It was a waste perhaps, but not of much.

A recent occupant of minor office who was even then an elder statesman and whose (involuntary) waste was very great is Neil Marten. Harold Wilson, an accomplished virtuoso in the Commons, was, in his first term as Prime Minister, worried about only two Tory back-benchers—John Peyton and Neil Marten. Why Peyton, a mannered and fey little pocket orator, should have worried anyone I do not understand. But Marten was a wit, without spite or nastiness and, improbably in the Conservative Party, a man of conviction.

Alas, it was the wrong conviction, humorous observation of the imperfection of the Common Market. He was also in those days something of a sceptic about overseas aid. He was passed over by Mr Heath; and, later, the whips, who arrange these things, made him, for Mrs Thatcher, Minister of State at the Foreign Office in charge of Overseas Aid, which is rather like putting an actuary in charge of a slush fund. He died in the House. The jokes and the zest went, he seems permanently tired and dispirited, not least by jet lag as he was shot from Caracas to Bangkok. The Tory Party is notoriously short of intelligent, independent-minded men and at a loss what to do with those it has. Marten would have done better to have stayed snapping two inches below the surface of the Nile than, in minor office, to have become the most elegant of handbags. He is too intelligent to have been Minister of State at the Foreign Office.

Not that the lifting of responsibility soothes everyone's temper. David Ennals, who was Minister of Health under the last Government, enjoys a vigorous retirement but rather in the way of those imperious grandpas who have ruined many a childhood. He has, oddly, most of Mrs Thatcher's faults. Does she hector, is she overbearing, intolerant, preoccupied with an issue, moralistic? Mr Ennals is all of these. He talks to the House as if it had forgotten its gym kit again. And there is a sort of sullen persistence about the man. He has something important to say and people ought to listen to it. No, he won't make way this time, he has been very good as it is. How people cannot understand a point so obvious astounds him. He aims at, but does not quite reach, asperity; but at the prolonged moan he has few serious competitors. When he was Minister. . . .

There is a lot of that in the Republic of the Dead. But it is not all resentful self-pity. Hard-bitten, closely reasoned speeches of the kind which are rarely reported are made. Douglas Jay on defence, indeed on most things, is a good illustration. Mr Jay missed being Chancellor. But his criticisms of the Government are, with those of Mr Joel Barnett, the most effective it has to bear. They are so precisely because, unlike Mr Healey, these two are not looking over their shoulders at the party faithful. They never did like rhetoric very much nor conference podiums, but in the cool of a late afternoon, putting their own private views, they can be the very devil.

Jay annoys the Left of his Party by putting the nuclear defence case quite simply better than anybody else. He uses no jargon, is better educated than a man of equivalent talent twenty-five years younger and speaks English. Jay on defence—strong, coherent and unexcited—is a ghostly reminder of what the Labour Party used to be like at the top. With his stick-like body, cracked-oboe voice, radar-screen ears and his cautious Keynesianism, Jay was always the best of Hugh Gaitskell's group, the late Anthony Crosland not excepted. He is stupendously frugal: 'What will you have? I'm having the set meal myself.' This to a devoted constituency worker in a Battersea café after a day's canvassing. But he is meticulous and rigorous. Nothing is done for smartness, nothing for fashion. The younger Jay may be Intellect-in-Residence to Breakfast TV, his father applies cerebral punctilio on a parade-ground where undone buttons, straggling puttees and round shoulders are the norm. He is the exact Don in politics.

Joel Barnett, of the now disbanded firm of Sheldon, Barnett and Dell, devaluers of the pound before circumstances devalued it for them in 1967, is another of the elder glories. He has the faintest of giggles, presumably authorized to chartered accountants when contemplating the broad folly of things as they are done by people who can't count. Barnett of course was the brains behind Denis Healey's cleverness. He is inexcusably cheerful, perhaps with the knowledge of a job well done. It was the Healey–Barnett regime which, however embarrassing this may be now, gave us two solid Peelite, cost-cutting, debt-reducing years of fiscal conservatism. They came after the two years of treating money as a metaphysical abstraction and after the Chancellor had performed the ultimate U-turn ... in his car at the airport. They also took place before a very human attempt to win the election. But, as Mr Barnett justly claims, he cut more than his Conservative successor; and, as Mr Barnett fairly concedes, there was more to cut. It leaves us with 1976 rather than 1979 as the hinge of economic and financial policy in this country. Barnett, like his profession, is about arithmetic. In consequence he made a number of speeches in office which Mrs Thatcher has a fondness for quoting, so close do they come to her own injunctions. Barnett has to dance out of all this somehow, which he does by generally deploring the Government's judgement and competence. He is a loyal Labour man who simply did the necessary.

Joel Barnett gives the impression of being a happy man. He chairs the Public Accounts Committee which examines waste in public spending. As someone remarked of a public hangman, he gives the impression of enjoying his work. The press, I believe, slips up in not covering these reports with more zest and vigour. The PAC is limited of course by being an after-the-event tribunal. First the Government and civil servants waste a sum of money, then, when it has all happened, the PAC in one of its invaluable papers, points the fact out. Even so my instinct is that a decently bloody-minded news editor splashing the PAC vigorously enough could get chlorinated water all over some very discreet public figures. Most bank robberies have occurred before they come to court. Prime space and time for the PAC, so that negligent men with power—the Pottingers of omission—were made to sweat for yesterday's misallocations and think harder about this year's options, would be a public good. One could see Sir Peter Middleton, Mrs Thatcher's waste-hating new Treasury Under-Secretary, welcoming it.

Barnett is a nice man, small, neat, with the intellectual breadth of the more conservative sort of Manchester Jewish professional and business man. He brings a breath of Cheatham Hill, or at any rate Didsbury, to a chamber which tends to think in terms of South or North. If it is ever necessary to suspend Mr Livingstone, metaphorically that is, Barnett would make an excellent District Commissioner for Greater London.

Geographically far more remote, but socially just another Etonian, is Jo Grimond, the last Liberal leader but one, who has announced his retirement from Parliament. Nobody is against Grimond outside the Liberal Party, to whose traditional policies he adheres. For Mr Grimond, despite the conversion of his party into a prigs' crusade, remains a non-interventionist, a believer in the market, in free intelligence and a free economy, but he is always so charming about this that his busy, moralizing colleagues find it difficult to believe he really exists.

He has a voice which is wispy and tentative in contrast to his views which are as tentative as Leeds Town Hall. He is to be blamed for one thing though, the subjection of us all to the word 'radical', as in 'radical new departures' used to signify 'nothing very much'. Perhaps he has a legitimate claim on it (in the terms of 1860), being an unreconstructed old Cobdenite himself, but on the lips of Mr Steel or Mr Jenkins 'radical' sounds like a call to the barricades from the Savoy. Grimond sits where he does more or less by choice, having given himself ten years to make the Liberal Party succeed and having decided that he had not done so, though he certainly caused it to be taken seriously for the first time since the 1929 manifesto. He not only jumped when he left; he was asked later to climb up again, his successor, Mr Thorpe, having been acquitted with no stain on his character for alleged conspiracy to murder. The Liberals, forced otherwise to decide the precedence between David Steel and John Pardoe, begged Grimond to come back. Cincinnatus wisely stayed where he was.

His interventions are philosophic; but a broad endorsement emerges of the sort of thinking which moves Mr Biffen, Sir Geoffrey and Mrs Thatcher. He actually dislikes government; and sceptical melancholy is never far away. He has been touched by personal tragedy, the death of his son; compassion always seems to belong with him. He stands, of course, in relation to dreadful little Steel like wood to plastic.

Not everyone can be a philosopher. Mr St John-Stevas, touched upon lightly elsewhere, is in an exile he did not choose, and, more to the point, did not expect. For, like Grimond, Stevas is an amateur, however hard he may have worked on editing Bagehot's encyclopaedia of platitudes or on the new committee system. He is an amateur in not knowing when to shut up. Only those with serious working memories can remember how well placed he once was and indeed how funny his speeches used to be. He was Leader of the House, the star Conservative speaker, the one politician whom people not otherwise interested in politics had heard of. There was nothing damaging about his showbiz associations; nor was it an absolute liability to run stunts like the harp in the bathroom or the grave plot in Rome.

Politicians may or may not, in the words of the canvassed householder, 'be in it for themselves'. The trouble with Stevas was that he seemed to be entirely in it *about* himself. The little jokes about compliments he had received were perhaps meant as a self-send-up but they sounded like old Norman adjusting his tie in front of the mirror and getting on everybody's nerves. Without becoming serious he stopped being funny. Ironically, now that he is Out, hurt and unhappy about it all, he does attempt a grave style on the back benches. And one begins to see his trouble. Once asked to do a Matthew Arnold and 'be always wholly earnest', he is compelled to do it by numbers. The sort of dull, responsible speech which, from a master like Barney Heyhoe comes out like spaghetti on a production line, is an agony for him—safe and proper things to say, modest but loyal criticism, and solid worth. And his calls at conference for 'One Nation' were limp, unfearful things. Hope of the Speaker's chair is possibly spoiling his retirement. If he were to go on to open blade he could make a very sharp speech indeed, instead he hangs between hope and despair, trying to pick up discretion, a lady of advanced years and castellated virtue. It would be nice if he cheered up and went back to the jokes.

Among the Dead must be counted former Ministers of State who show little sign of becoming Ministers of State again. Mr Alexander Lyon of York is one of these. A small, swarthy man with gold-rimmed spectacles and a sense of humour which has lost heavily on points to his sanctimoniousness, he was eliminated Chicago-style by his smiling leader within hours of Mr Callaghan taking office to cries of,

'This is happening because I have tried to help black people.' Not for the first time the Tories are softer on an issue than machine Labour. Just as Labour played Northern Ireland with no illusions (whereas James Prior has tried to build an ice castle in hell), so Callaghan's view of immigration was that a lot of it went a long way. He was concerned that Mr Lyon, a compulsive Zimbabwean freedom fighter and well-wisher of Indian fiancés, should go further.

Recently Mr Callaghan was speaking about some aspect of penal policy. Alex Lyon, with a low moan from just in front of him, said *sotto voce*, 'You sent me to Siberia.' 'The Honourable Gentleman is mistaken,' said Uncle Jim. 'I didn't send him to Siberia. I sacked him.' And he knew what he was doing. Lyon was more than an ordinary humanitarian, he was a bad case of what George Orwell called 'transferred nationalism'. He did not so much like immigrants and some of the more regrettable African political movements as give the impression of disliking England.

He was also in trouble of a mild sort ten years ago in his delightful constituency of York on account of his devotion to the EEC. Indeed there is a good deal of the closet Social Democrat about Lyon, who was a supporter of Roy Jenkins. And one is surprised to find that Mr Foot, who is anxious to stretch the fabric of the Party's donkey jacket as far as it will go, has not invited so apparently congenial a figure back on to the front benches. He would make an admirable moderate for display purposes while holding excitable views only on topics which excite Mr Foot himself. But Mr Lyon, despite qualification and relative political youth (he is only 51) is *not* congenial. He attracts dislike, not least by a Holy Willy character which seems to thank God that he is not as other men. Other men have been known to say much the same thing.

Similar problems face Mr Robert Rhodes James, who, as he has not yet held office and is no more than on the elderly side of young will not care to be included here. Yet Mr Rhodes James, related though he is to M. R. James, the writer of ghost stories (the family did not then affect a second barrel to its name), was floated at an unrealistic price. He is one of those men who do remarkable things in their youth and then fade. He was known as the biographer of Lord Randolph Churchill. He early held an important post connected with the United Nations; people used vaguely to approve of the United Nations but from today's vantage point it might have been wiser to have held an important post in the Salvation Army. He was also, in his busy way, once one of the clerks of the House. Rumour proclaims that he expected office as soon as the Government was elected, regarding himself as exceptionally qualified. Mrs Thatcher has resisted the temptation. And one does not see James, lank haired, heavily serious and devoted to the great blank office in Turtle Bay, really stirring her matter-of-factly 'What about the British?' cast of mind to enthusiasm. And while one can see the usual sort of whip urging his case—'Outstandingly able, Prime Minister'—at 48 he has always managed to sound like a former Minister. The 'When I was ...' technique makes no friends. It is quite painful enough when it comes from people who *have* had a Ministry to get wrong. And Mr James has so great an hauteur, not being quite sure whether he is a scholar, a bureaucrat or an MP, that he does not move the lads on the shop floor to spontaneous cries of 'Give Rhodes James a job.' He has so far been omitted and looks entirely omissible.

More fun than Rhodes James, since the pomposity is more or less intended, is Nicholas Fairbairn, dearer to the tabloid press than any Scottish Solicitor-General in history. His tactic, like Stevas's, is a cod conceit. He speaks in the manner of a politician accustomed to rub shoulders with Sir William Harcourt or Sir Michael Hicks-Beach. He dresses Victorian in three-piece suits of a peculiar cut which represent a fairly high point of sartorial atrocity, wears an Albert, something not seen in the House since A. V. Alexander was a rising man, and speaks in a high, fluting manner which leaves Roy Jenkins sounding like the man in the street. As we have all been told by that pooled dispatch which makes up the gossip columns, he lives in a Scottish castle, had a girl friend try ineffectively to kill herself for love of him (which, given his resemblance to a shifty marmoset, says wonders for the force of personality). He was brought down by rape—failure to prosecute over it, that is. The House has always attracted dressers-up and other actorish people as a small sideline. They used to have a wonderful time over the Budget in top hats and gardenias. Now, of the Florid Tendency, if you discount Brotherton's awful shirts, only Fairbairn and Abse are left. Abse, as remarked, is obsessed with Freudian analysis; Fairbairn is the son of a psychoanalyst!

He is a clever little man. Quite what he would have been like if he had turned his brisk talents from the legal profession and the affectation of oddness, one hesitates to think. A Fairbairn serious about politics might have hit us like a Moss Trooper on the loose.

His fellow Scot, Sir Ian Gilmour, has always taken life fairly grimly, as befits a man with a great deal to lose. He is quite furious with himself for having waited to be sacked in the September Massacres of 1981 when he had wanted to go much earlier as a resigner-in-protest. Mrs Thatcher had similar intentions and would have saved him the trouble in January of that year but for the intervention of Lord Carrington.

Sir Ian has excited derision in Dry circles over his books, but while the second of them, *Inside Right*, did read embarrassingly like an anthology of quotations, worn rather like the decorative embroidery of a pearly king (and showing the author unaware of the disappearance of the inside right from the formation of a football team in and about the year 1965), his first and better book was interesting and the coherent exposition of a reputable if mistaken case.

In the House, following his exile, he has not attracted much attention or thrown many bricks. This may be a temperamental thing—his best rows are private ones—and he is cursed with a public manner about as exciting as a paper cup. Yet he ought to be the centre of opposition. He is more intelligent than Prior and in a different league to a tide-born relic like Pym. But intellectual rigour makes for difficulties. Although we continue with all the problems of unemployment, his case for reflation by £5 billion 'tested on the Treasury model' has sounded less attractive since it was tested on the model of the French economy. The essential battle which he and his friends lost was the 1981 Budget.

The root of Sir Ian's thinking lies in anxiety. What is called progressive, liberal, or left-wing conservatism is only in part the product of R. A. Butler's positive beliefs in provision and welfare; it is also motivated by the panic which affected the Conservatives after 1945. Very privileged men were worried that their privileges were endangered and their possessions under threat. Their reaction is best seen in the weak and emollient policies practised towards the trade unions and their feckless response to inflation when it was moving up the foothills. But such policies, whatever uncompetitive prices they created, however much long-term trouble from unions pushing at open doors, were for the future. And the great moral flaw which runs through pragmatic, progressive Conservatism is that it has very little thought for the morrow. 'Will it see my time out?' is the self-damning approach. It is unequipped to do anything difficult even when it is still easy. Accordingly the difficulties grow more complex and chromatic and the return to some sort of rough rectitude more painful to accomplish.

There is something else. Progressive Conservatism needed growth quite as much as the Crosland–Gaitskell version of socialism. The standard answer to sharp questions in the late fifties was 'It will come out of growth . . .' which in our case we have not got.

There is also a matter of temperament. The sort of Conservative of whom Sir Ian is a highly intelligent representative has a distaste for conflict. Labour, once it had conquered its own early inferiority complex, has always been better at rough politics and at the exploitation of a moral point. The Tories are short of moral courage. Until they got a woman leader they frequently made up the feminine and passive component of politics. Sir Ian, who is fond of the rather damning quotation 'Whatever is, is right', would argue that this is part of a long tradition of wise accommodation. It depends what you are accommodating. The adjustment of the nineteenth-century Conservative Party to the broad franchise is not a justification for falling in with inflation, union privilege, the closed shop and a health and local government caste of administrators who have replaced Cobbett's tax-eaters. Sir Ian's pragmatism is geared to the acceptance of the least immediately painful form of defeat.

Such passivity, however well expounded on the printed page, is not geared to resisting force when it comes from the other direction. Mrs Thatcher was a shock horror never wholly taken in. Sir Ian got excitedly angry with her because he regarded her as an agent of left-wing strength. And he is perhaps more hostile, certainly more apprehensive of the Far Left than she is. There is a touch of the Apocalyptic in the man, and he takes the Screaming Left as seriously as they do themselves. This in turn makes him a social ameliorator, which is fine, except that in terms of power politics such concession-making is always grasped and understood by union and left-wing opponents as social appeasement. The unions were, after all, at their most militant and destructive when most was being conceded to them. The pity is that Sir Ian, for all the political philosophy he has read, seems not to have attended closely enough to Machiavelli:

> Upon this a question arises: whether it be better to be loved than feared or feared than loved? It may be answered that one should wish to be both, but, because it is difficult to unite them in one person, it is much safer to be feared than loved when of the two either must be dispensed with ... friendships that are obtained by payments ... may indeed be earned but they are not secured. ...

Sir Ian has been quiet on the back benches. He is often drily amusing and not precisely a bad speaker, but his manner always suggests the great patrician which he is not. Rather he is an enormously wealthy man, the patron in his shy way of the *Spectator*. But for a grandee he is insecure, with something of a King Ethelred complex.

There is also unmistakable social tension between him and Mrs Thatcher. Her first cabinet for the want of Airey Neave's guiding hand, was loaded to the gunwales with conventional panic-and-reflation Tories. They found her difficult, which she is. They also found her socially absurd, a counter-jumper, someone who should have been wearing a flowered hat and giving one of their sort a standing ovation at Conference. The role of pure British snobbery in the make-up of the leading Wets cannot be overstated. Admittedly Mr Heath came from below the salt, and he was not altogether easy either, but Heath after 1971 was very much the sergeant with a commission learning to react the way real officers do. Mrs Thatcher, despite the royal blue at Conference time and all the superficialities, is from a different social class and not prepared to be assimilated. She also thrives on conflict, which Gilmour for one is not good at. He rages semi-privately about the awfulness of the Government; but it is a Government in which he started strong (not least in her personal regard for him) and finished weak. It is no great affront to say that he is not a very good politician. At a guess, Sir Ian, who has an increasingly cool relationship with his constituency—Chesham and Amersham—is a candidate for a late-in-the-day retirement announcement. Given his views, he could have played a stronger, subtler hand in or out of office. He knows this and can only rage at his own want of finesse.

Altogether different in his last term is Angus Maude, the former organizer of Party PRO or 'Communications', as it is called in the language of PRO. A man of sardonic reticence, good at killing you dead with an eyebrow, Maude, even in retirement, is not a back number. He has the Prime Minister's ear, having been fired on public demand for not being a thrusting young dynamo. One has only to look at most of the thrusting young dynamos to see his continuing attraction. He is a melancholy, perceptive unbeliever who talks like rustling parchment. He is something of a minimalist, never very impressed by wonderful new schemes. He has also handled the Prime Minister in the sort of straightforward, civil but uncourtierly way she likes, saying yea or nay on his judgement. He is in consquence rather more influential out of office than in it and under no obligation to spend his time on the back benches in plaintive resentment, something for which he has no taste anyway.

Talk of plaintive resentment brings us inexorably to Mr Edward Heath. He is perpetually embarrassed by the example set by Sir Alec Douglas-Home, an example of how to keep what you really want, enjoy yourself, look serene and leave reshufflers grinding their teeth. For Sir Alec, never saying a word against his successor, quietly took what he could not be denied, the Foreign Office, and gave every sign of enjoying himself for the whole of Mr Heath's Prime Ministership—more than could be said for most of us.

If the reader casts his mind back to the events of 1975 and reads the contemporary comment, he will find the great recurring theme that there should be reconciliation and that, if Mr Heath sought the portfolio of any great office of state, except the Exchequer, it would be impossible for Mrs Thatcher to refuse it. This was not a circumstance narrowly confined to 1975; a rest before re-entry would have been entirely understood. And indeed 'Ted's job' continued to be talked about until well into 1978. Sedulous friends and choreographers laid on public reconciliations in the best, most spurious traditions of the party. It is banal to say that he was his own worst enemy, but banality and Mr Heath are hard to keep apart. He sulked, he struck attitudes. He took to parodying his aloofness by declining fully to attend his own Party Conferences, striking camp in some small neighbouring town—St Anne's for Blackpool and Lewes for Brighton, a portable St Germaine. A small court would be set up with favoured persons being summoned to dinners and lunches. In terms of working politics it is an approach quite unimaginably silly, advertising as it does to the world a piqued man's inability to contain his pique.

Heath's whole conduct in opposition has been one of self-destruction. The worst of all imaginable things could happen to the Prime Minister, from political catastrophe to death, and there will be nothing, unless it is a Bahamian embassy, for Mr Heath. *Aut Caesar aut nihil* is all very well but *nihil* it is. But at all times Mr Heath has been anything from bad to unspeakable at human relationships. When the challenge to his leadership came in 1975, his friend from business, Peter Walker, hurried about organizing coffee mornings for Members 'to meet Ted'. As one of the MPs put it, by way of a Clem Attlee one-line annihilator, 'Bit late, isn't it?'

Jeffrey Archer tells the story of how as a newly elected Conservative MP in 1970 he smiled wanly at his leader, only to be walked through, while Harold Wilson running, a little puffed, for the division lobby called out to Archer, a former University sprinter, 'You're better built for this than I am, Jeffrey.' A little touch of Harold in the evening. If it is alleged that Mr Heath stood aloof from the petty camaraderie and small ingratiations of politics, the more fool him. The Commons is an essentially amiable place, where it is a necessary but not always sufficient requirement to treat less important people with civility and friendliness.

Disregard for the moment the errors and miscalculations of the Heath Government. Rationally Mr Heath, a seemingly strong, not unintelligent man, surrounded largely by hand-picked supporters and *in situ*, should have been bomb-proof against his Minister of Education. Look at the other leadership changes: Sir Alec went out of diffidence; Mr Macmillan from panic about his health; Eden out of real ill health and manifest catastrophe; Churchill from old age and semi-consent. They were each of them replaced by a number two or number three man. Even with his immediate mistakes and General Election defeat, how did Heath come to record 119 votes against the 130 of his number twelve?

Heath is the father of Margaret Thatcher. No half-shrewd, middlingly well liked political leader would have been vulnerable, even after a succession of very serious mistakes in government, to such an outsider's pitch. But then some of his trouble came from the fact that he was, and very self-consciously so, an outsider himself. He had been cruelly mocked as 'the Grocer'. He is the son of a skilled craftsman turned small builder, just as Mrs Thatcher is the daughter of a factory worker turned shopkeeper. We do not in England yet glory that such ascents can be made. The putting of people down by amused allusion to their origins, the fatuous giggle which can be had free by referring to a London outer suburb or a working town in the North is a flaw at the heart of us despite the fact that outsiders do rise.

In consequence, Mr Heath, who rose by written examinations and ferocious concentration of purpose, became a slightly unreal man. His well-known over-esteem for the Civil Service had something to do with it being, or seeming in a bad light to be, a meritocracy. He also became extravagantly official and thus remote in his dealings, something not helped by long years in the whips' office at a time when obedience was more widely expected than it is now. Again he was reacting against Harold Wilson, whose affability and taste for easy options seemed intolerable to Heath: the showbiz parties, the Humber Bridge, the flight to oversee the *Torrey Canyon*. Wilson had brought popularity into disrepute. Heath meant to put that right. 'Man of Principle', said the poster from which Mr Heath looked out like Diocletian in a nice suit. Principle, so far as the Commons was concerned, was to mean a personal stiffness and a way of talking like a combination of departmental memorandum and robot. And, alas, what we were watching was the simulated-implacability principle. To come back to Machiavelli, 'If you have to choose between being loved and being feared, get yourself feared.' But if the fear breaks down, affection is a very tolerable spare wheel.

And Heath's trouble was that while he needed to be a strong man for his whole act to stay together, he was nothing of the sort. His Prime Ministership was littered with flight and retreat: Upper Clyde Shipbuilders; the Official Solicitor and the five dockers; the concession under French pressure of a Common Fishing Policy which has destroyed the British fishing fleet at a stroke; the taking on of the miners and the running away from the miners; and finally, most important of all, the collapse of nerve when a figure of 1 million unemployed was touched. Harold Wilson, who has great felicity in opposition, called it the U-turn.

Yet Heath is still in a simmering rage that anyone in the present Government should criticize his record. Regularly rising from his ex-Prime Minister's seat below the gangway to attack this Government, he demands total loyalty to the record of *his* Administration. It is all very sad. He did not know how to win and gives a regular demonstration that he does not know how to lose. He sits impatiently, pasha-like, intimating a remote indication to Mr Speaker that he be heard at once, something with which that sweet soul complies. Those speeches are a grave mistake for they lead him to lose his nerve again in shadow form. Most people were in favour of the Falklands expedition, some were honourably against it from the start. Only Mr Heath suggested that we had been right to set out, but that having got into the southern hemisphere we should regard that as our necessary accomplishment and turn back.

Perhaps the real trick to the lock of Mr Heath's mind is his Civil Service background. The U-turns would not startle a civil servant. Mr Heath's principle was of executive leadership, of decisions and counter-decisions to accommodate necessity, while the public minded their own business. Good politics has something to do with talking to people and persuading them.

It wasn't an accident that Heath was a very poor performer in the chamber. His failure as a House of Commons man, like his war on the English language, is an oblique indicator of what is wrong. The Commons, for all its set pieces, predictable votes and bogus riots, is a thoroughly human place and it is a market in the flair and talent of working politicians. If you can, you do; if you can't, you dismiss it as irrelevant. Heath never could get across. He can make a Handelian 'major speech', but it will be a unilateral affair, a reading into the record by someone with little more respect for Parliament than Mr Benn.

The word 'democrat' always turns a little curdled on Mr Heath's tongue. He had, and has, a passion for 'massive' (his favourite word) government action; he brooked no dissension inside his cabinet, believed more in the Civil Service than anyone since Hegel—and a good deal more than the best civil servants do; he was a sublime élitist.

But at the end of all Mr Heath's massive responses lay his own Civil Service taste for cancelling the draft of a policy as if it were not already launched, spoken for, adhered to, deemed by some even to be a principle.

He *hates* the Government, has ever fewer sympathizers among those who share his views, and exists in the Commons like a sulk made flesh. Even those of us who do not care for the word, begin to feel towards him something approaching compassion. He is a one-man Bourbon, a legitimist—comfortably taken care of with the profits of wise speculation and the sale of two preposterous books. He even has therapy in the form of the Brandt Commission, but no serenity.

Yet none of his misfortunes came from a deeply adventurous policy. He was the apostle of the received wisdom—incomes policies, reflation, *dirigisme*, the outlook of a latter-day Colbert. And indeed 'Mon ami Edouard', as M. Pompidou called him, subsidizer of continental over-production, signer-away of the British fishing fleet, dismisser of all questions of sovereignty, never seemed quite to belong in his own country.

The other ex-Prime Ministers are nothing like as much trouble. Indeed the difficulty with Sir Harold is to get a view of him. There was a speech about cable and wireless so complicated that I for one didn't understand it, but for the most part Sir Harold has settled for a benign discretion, only ever being mischievous on television. Apart from recommending Mr Benn for the Directorship of London Zoo, he seems to try to be nice about people. His own bruises in government have made him willing to see the best in other Governments and to express a quiet melancholy at the chances of anybody getting it right. For the most tremendous showman in office, his quietness now is startling. Nothing, nothing at all is done to fire off thunderflashes and say, 'I'm here, I'm here.' It is as if the rushing around the film set of the Prime Ministership has left him with a scepticism so profound that he does not care to voice it. Also Sir Harold, despite his sharpness in debate and excessive tendency to see plots when he was Prime Minister, is a kind man. Knocks on the head are strictly for the jousting lists and he has grown tired of tournaments. 'Nothing extenuate, nor set down aught in malice' seems to be the guiding principle now. He was also once a civil servant, but what he seems to have learnt in that trade, for the latter part of his career, is not massive intervention, but an unbelieving discretion. He was, in office, recurringly compared with Walter Mitty. I suspect, and it is only a personal view, that the events of 1967–8, the devaluation against which he had set his mind and the frustration of 'In Place of Strife' broke most of his real enthusiasm. Wilson is a very intelligent man with a full grasp of what ought to be done. Behind a lot of rather flash activity his instinct was to do good by stealth—the only course in the Labour Party. A major reform of whose necessity the next decade was to give a torchlit demonstration, was defeated by a combination of the Left and the machine politicians. Surprise electoral defeat in 1970 must have battered him further, but the real embittering experience may have been the union requirement, now forgotten, to oppose the Howe Industrial Relations Bill with the massed hysteria of Irish Members in the 1880s, guillotined clauses being voted on, one tediously after another, division bell after division bell, at the end of the committee stage.

Peter Jenkins quotes him as having said to Mr Scanlon at the height of the 'In Place of Strife' struggle, which occurred at roughly the same time as the Soviet invasion of Czechoslovakia, 'Get your tanks off my lawn, Hughie.' Sir Harold owes the Labour Party much, as it does him, and he will do nothing to embarrass it. That silence is, if one thinks about it, remarkably eloquent.

Mr Callaghan is not silent. He is, as so often in his earlier career, a judicious intervener on the winning side. The Callaghan Falklands speech may have come from the heart if there is any such place. It grasped the mood of the time in a way which the toiling Foreign Minister proved himself incapable of. Its conclusion, 'God speed', which warmed the more ingenuous spirits opposite, was only the latest of a series of nautical metaphors going back to 'blown off course' in 1967. It was duly followed with a low punch months later when the Falklands inquiry was debated and the Member for Cardiff South-East, watching another audience this time, demanded Mrs Thatcher's resignation.

My uncharity does not imply a lack of respect. Mr Callaghan is the most accomplished professional politician in the House. In so far as he has convictions they are a very long way to the Right and the populist working-class Right at that. He is not a natural *Guardian* reader but he is the child of deprivation, if those two things are not indeed antitheses. He is a former NCO in the Navy, more than something of a bully, and he has made a modest fortune.

But never deny that accomplishment of his. The back-bench interventions are invariably of the highest order, funny, pertinent, clever and carefully judged to obtain a serious reception even from his opponents. Callaghan is only nominally in the House of the Dead. His speeches have very little of the 'I remember when I was Prime Minister/Home Secretary/Chancellor of the Exchequer' stuff about them. They are addressed to the day, though it was a sour notion for the Home Secretary, whose intrusion arguably broke the dike in Northern Ireland, to be dropping deft hints that 'Troops out' might be a good idea. Mr Callaghan spoke without reflection on the Lebanon which has a thing or two to teach Ulster.

Even so there have been times, in poor Mr Foot's wretched demonstration of how not to lead a parliamentary opposition, when the former leader has come close to holding him up. Callaghan is nothing if not a complete professional. He can make the speech Foot should have made, attacking the Government in quiet, measured, reasonable terms, using anger like a judiciously applied condiment, where the good-natured Foot treats nuance as if it were something newfangled, invented after 1955. As pure politics the Callaghan interventions are very good. And the thought has crossed more than one mind that the ablest, least nice politician of our times is making availability noises, that there might be some sort of comeback.

He is a year older than Foot, but he is a vigorous Reaganesque 70 to Foot's stricken, antiquarian 69. It can't really happen and there is a vast difference between the most energetic life after office and the full-time, rather dreary job of leading an Opposition. But he must take satisfaction from his obvious superiority as a parliamentarian, not only to Foot but to all the Aspirants: Kinnock, a clever, nice talkative youngster; Hattersley, moving into the realms of self-parody; Denis Winston, noisy, bombastic and without timing. Only

Callaghan really knows the stops on this pipe and can make it play. Most elder statesmen make you wonder betwixt whimpering and reminiscence why they were in office in the first place. Only Callaghan, dislike him as one does, leaves us with the question of why he ever left.

Yet he was about as disloyal to Wilson, even allowing for a difference of judgement over trade union reform, as it was possible to be, because he acknowledged with simple other-worldly cynicism in the power of those unions to smash anything in sight and to make him Prime Minister. The Italian philosopher to whom I have alluded would have liked Uncle Jim, but then the great admiration of Machiavelli's life was Cesare Borgia.

As a back-bench elder statesman he is benevolent, good humoured, avuncular and has no illusions. He is the chocolate with the iron-ore filling. Harold Wilson always wanted to be loved. Callaghan at the very least was better liked than any post war Prime Minister, Churchill apart, and stood in no such need. We got a glimpse of Iago as Doge, and very good at it he was.

9

The Four Just Persons

As one writes Mr Benn is having as unrewarding a time as any Hong Kong property stock. He has been removed from his offices within the Labour Party, including the Chairmanship of the Home Policy Committee. He has been very ill—a tribulation put down by serious drinking men to over-indulgence in tea, something which did for Edgar Wallace. And unfortunately for this account, he has not anyway been a great House of Commons presence for some time.

Long before he was ill, Mr Benn had begun to treat the Commons as a very great nuisance, intrinsically less important than a Tribune meeting in St Pancras Town Hall, a nuclear disarmament rally or any gathering of the People.

Benn in the House is like Pontius Pilate but less succinct. He does not stay for an answer either, but, instead of putting an unanswerable question to the followers of the new cult, he makes a speech at once short and interminable. There is more of Mr Heath in Wedgie than meets the eye—a certain spoilt querulousness, a resentment of argument or interruption, however civil, and a preoccupation only slightly less drastic than Heath's with himself. The speech comes out in that peeved voice and whether it is the thunder of the absurd—military coup at the hands of the Chief Constables—or the drizzle of his more cautious propositions, it is a set piece. Benn has enormous facility as a speaker but no talent for debate. And when polite intervenors do get in, the quality of his riposte is very poor, often not much better than a 'That's as may be, however I must be getting on' sort of answer.

And he does not stay. He will occupy the end seat above the gangway, will wait fretfully through the superfluities of others, will

claim his full Privy Councillor's right to jump the queue, make his
declamation and have done with us. They are not for the most part
successful speeches, partly because nobody speaks at his best to a
hostile audience: and dislike of Mr Benn goes beyond the Tories,
beyond what is even called the Labour Right to a radical working-
class element which can't stand the sight of him. Secondly, Benn
fails because, like Michael Heseltine whom he so resembles, his
style of address is old-fashioned. But while Heseltine has the
advantage of public business to muffle his Roland at Roncevalles
posture, Benn, in opposition to Opposition, does not. And the great
thing about the Commons as an audience is its very high boiling-
point. The public has been upset, it is true, by the noisiness of
Question Time. But this is a combination of quite phoney show and
the serious activity of the thicker element, still a well-contained
minority in this mixed-ability school. For the most part, order
papers are waved at the end of limp wrists and real admiration for a
strong, clever speech is measured in a pleased murmur. Benn keeps
on making speeches better designed for his public than for highly
sophisticated technicians. Even were Mr Arthur Scargill himself to
step into the House of Commons he would have a very thin time.
MPs being themselves in the forensic business and knowing the
standard crowd-wowing levers and buttons, are in consequence
quite unwowable. Mr Scargill, like Mr Benn, would waste his
sweetness on the desert air.

Having had this experience a good many times, not without
sending reporters scurrying from the gallery to their telephones
with that useful claim to the front page, 'Wedgie's gone bananas
again', Mr Benn now cultivates disdain. A Commons speech made
in uncongenial company is something to be got through, rather like
a tour of the estate. And as Mr Benn moves further and further to
the political equivalent of rick-firing, so does his manner acquire
ever more of the Antarctic qualities of a highland-clearing duke.
And the speeches themselves are absurd beyond the dreams of
Richard Wagner: oil he has described as 'my legacy to the Prime
Minister'; Keynes was too authoritarian for his taste; the trade
unions should prepare themselves for the great role they would be
playing with management on joint committees in regenerating
investment; trade should be planned and if this meant delays in
obtaining goods we should recall that it takes some time to lay on
cold surgery in the Health Service. The image of a British export
economy operating along the lines of an NHS waiting list, with the
unions deciding what is and is not urgent, is more amusing in Milan
and Taipei than it is here. All of that was in a single speech. In
another he accused the media of using the language of *Mein Kampf*
in our little differences of opinion with the trade unions.

He denounced the bankers' conspiracy which had imposed cuts

on the Government of which he was a member; 'and stayed on,' said someone nastily. He also talked speculatively about the police; designs for their future uniforms reminding him of the SAS. Benn does not ever quite *say* the wildest things he imputes by innuendo. But a picture of a government operating South American style, first crushing the workers and then suppressing them, is built up. It is immeasurably silly, not because the Conservative Government is a fountain of light and goodness, but because the smear is outside the range of belief. Much better politics it is, from a working Labour point of view, to call Mrs Thatcher thick-headed, wrong, a hard-hearted, posh lady in an electric-blue suit. That is relatively to the point, to call her a South American General putting down the peasantry lacks conviction.

While we are about it, this Fleet Street conspiracy is interesting. It is quite true that the owners of newspapers do not greatly like Mr Benn, but the sharper chicken has no profound regard for the poultry farmer. And so much has come from the Benn wing of the Labour Party in favour of censorship and the enforced carrying of hostile comment that Mr Benn can hardly complain if his Prime Ministership is seen by editors, never mind evil, black proprietors, as postponable. Benn gets attention because he behaves in and out of the House as if he wanted attention. It is no good alleging conspiracy on all hands and then resenting suggestions of paranoia. But on one point Mr Benn has justice on his side. Allegations are sometimes made that he is in some undefined way mentally unstable, and references are made to the quality of his eyes. This is malicious nonsense.

The problem is quite different. Mr Benn is very sane, but even more than the generality of politicians he has always loved publicity and prominence. One recalls him in his politically uncontroversial days before 1970, opening the atrocious Post Office Tower with a speech which recurringly referred to Big Ben. Cynically, the press concluded that he wanted the thing to be called Bigger Benn and disobliged. The itch of self is very great. In consequence he looks for short cuts. Although he is entirely capable of hard work and Departmental devotion, he has always responded, whether as a radical or as the regular Joe Cabinet, which he was in the sixties, to *marvellous solutions to all our problems*. Not for nothing was he a pioneer of Concorde, the rich man's De Lorean. His talk in those temperate days was only of 'the regeneration of Britain'. It was Sir Harold who made the ill-advised remark about the 'white heat of the technological society'. But it was Benn who most uncritically believed it.

To that end he was a believer in the bigness of business. It was he who played matchmaker between BMC and Leyland Motors and thus commenced a decade and more of British Leyland. Like Mr

Walker, he has never allowed actual failure in office to cloud the splendour of his career. But where Walker, having failed in local government, then set about the fish, Benn with a bankrupt aeroplane and a charge-account motor works behind him, turned his attentions to the workers.

His shift to the Left could be put down to a number of causes, not least the daft desire of parents to please their children. When the younger Benns went through a phase Benn joined it. It could be attributed to 1968, that flash of tropical politics in the nursery. It scared General de Gaulle into blind panic so why should it not captivate Benn like a box of fireworks let off at the bottom of the garden? It could be blamed on the influence of Mrs Carole Benn, a busy American lady whom some have found unendearing, or to a late reading of the romantic left-wing historians, Christopher Hill and E. P. Thompson; for Mr Benn's imagery was to become charged with reference to the Levellers, the Diggers and other marginal men of the English Commonwealth.

Now there was never anything dishonourable in this romantic Leftism; a love affair with the working class was after all the chief inspiration of George Orwell. But it was also another way of believing in short cuts. The irreversible transfer of whatever it was to the Workers was simply the White Heat of the Technological Revolution Mark 2. Although he can be devious in self-defence, ideas have to be fairly simple for Benn to grasp them. Some people like problems; Benn likes solutions, and he has this way of working back from them to show the iniquity of whatever is preventing the perfect solution from taking place. And it has varied from conspiracy of the multi-nationals, to the press using the language of *Mein Kampf*, to the bankers, the Special Patrol Group, Consolidated Perspex, the villain of your choice, but always some malign conspiracy.

And in the process Mr Benn has deteriorated. The chuckle-headed idealist we could all be very kindly towards—the 'Jimmy' of whom his old friend Anthony Crosland said, 'There's nothing fundamentally wrong with Jimmy except that he's a bit cracked'—has grown ill humoured and spiteful. And for a romantic friend of the people and opponent of power conspiracies, he has an unpleasing admiration for trade unions for the raw power they have.

The notorious 1972 'Liftmen' speech, when by innuendo he called for manual workers in newspapers to exercise censorship, was a power-worshipping affair and an ugly one. Benn was as fascinated by the strength of the unions in the days when they were taking twenty and thirty per cent wage increases, as he once was by gadgets and mergers.

Now there is an element on the Left, which is deeply exercised by and cares without pretence for the low-earner, the man in the poverty trap. The best of these people are moved simply by a concern for poor people. Given a difference in style and address, 'The Working Class' as against 'the Poor and Deprived', one would have expected Mr Benn to have close friends and allies there. He does not. If there is an illustration of his quiet genius for getting things wrong, it lies in the existence today of a split Left. Aneurin Bevan, the last alternative leader of the Labour Party, had no such problem, even at the most radical point in the graph of his opinion.

It was not just that Bevan was always able to excite affection. There was a lot of that going for 'Jimmy' once. It was not a matter of the choice of one's associates. (A very sinister bunch of people of a neo-Stalinist mentality, who naturally stood shoulder to shoulder with People's Democracy, tried to use Mr Bevan.) So, although it doesn't help to have Reg Race for an admirer, he isn't in the same league as the 1945 Comintern element. The dislike for Benn is, one concedes sadly, quite personal.

Affection for 'Jimmy' came largely from his own class. No more than Roy Jenkins can he truly get across to the working and lower middle classes. And it is rather depressing to be an unpopular populist. Not that being a gentleman and educated at Westminster School will do you any harm with the electorate who have a terrible reverence even for their dafter betters. It could even have been parleyed through the more sticky undergrowth of the Parliamentary Labour Party which is rather more democratic and nob-resentful. But Benn's passion for absolute solutions goes with a lordly and contemptuous manner. It has actually got worse. The slightly phoney but engaging fellow, who used to take his coat off and sit on the table with his legs dangling at *Socialist Commentary* meetings, talking (very convincingly I used to think), about the gap between prototypes and production, reminding us that the piano was invented in 1696 and the typewriter in 1714, has lost all that charm. He treats opponents either as villains, traitors or fools. He has also retreated into particularism and into the company of his admirers. What the Left was able to give Benn in the early seventies was an assurance of admiration, even adoration. One speaks of the importance of low motives in politicians but should not underestimate fundamentally childish ones. It was a Faustian relationship in which he had to give more and more for the delusion of getting something back in return. If one looks back to the early ascendancy of the Left ten years ago, when Jack Jones and Hugh Scanlon had semi-divine powers and when militancy, however tending, was the wave of the future (which it has been), his actions could have passed for good, low politics, though it is not the sort of combination people are much inclined to vote for.

As a result Benn gambled where a wiser man would have

dabbled. Ironically one can perfectly well see circumstances in which, by playing his cards differently, Benn might have finished as leader of the Labour Party. He was once in good standing with the members of the PLP, a bit naïve, given to enthusiasms, perhaps too professionally boyish. If he had been a real politician in the manner of Jim Callaghan, he would have let the Left get the occasional view of his ankle, he would have been radical in a broad, sympathetic sort of way. To be brutal, he would have used his talents to make himself look good but he would have stayed within the mainstream of the Parliamentary Party. The PLP did after all in 1980 elect just such a romantic, soft left-winger, Michael Foot, by way of a compromise despite all the anxieties caused by his age and lack of front-bench experience. How might not a rose-petal version of Wedgie, thirteen years younger and with twelve of them in the cabinet, have done? Pointless to say he would have attracted distrust. No politician worth consideration is not in some degree distrusted. But the old-style Benn, devoted to technology, adjusted a few degrees in favour of a mild leftism, and, most important of all, staying on civil terms with the Parliamentary Party, would arguably have been the best-placed compromise candidate to take the leadership in succession to Mr Callaghan. And it will not do for Mr Benn to eye such a prospect with the scorn of a man who is above advancement. He is, to put it temperately, as ambitious as a politician can be. Mr Foot defied office for years; Mr Heffer resigned from office; but Mr Wedgwood Benn did not miss a single day of cabinet rank from 1964 to 1970 and from 1974 to 1979.

So, without malice, one has to see an element of calculation in his decision to join the revolutionary circuit and make speeches which would guarantee him a hostile coverage from the Conservative press, which he saw as a positive asset, as well as gaining a ready-drilled regiment of admirers. This calculation, together with the foolish impatience which seeks total solutions, is the reason why Mr Benn is where he is today: three feet forward from nowhere. For, even if the Left surmounts its recent losses on the NEC, it is very doubtful if a man who has used and been used, has now much long-term utility to the Left. The lean, hard men from the GLC, who are our alternative future, have their own power structure, and while Mr Benn is a welcome guest artist, he is not part of it.

The thoughtful radicals, who work hard and long at the poverty trap, are desolated by him. We are back with Benn's essential defect: a mounting inability to keep people's affection. This, of course, more than calculation or than his passion for solutions, may have determined his change of outlook. When a man indicates his contempt for Parliament he is commonly expressing his inability either to make it work or to stay on friendly terms with the citizens of that good-humoured republic. In other words, Parliament has found him out as a human being, a pretty good argument for Parliament.

So many commentators have made us familiar with the fallacious notion of Mr Benn and Enoch Powell as the opposite points of excess that it is impossible now to kick against the clichés. But what tend to show these days are the differences. Whichever way the Labour Party goes, Benn is on a down spiral, withdrawn, bitter and increasingly wild. Mr Powell is nearer than he has been for a decade and a half to serenity.

Despite the affinity in their economic views, it was never likely that Mrs Thatcher would give Powell office, and he, who once wanted the exercise of power very much, has, at 70, come to terms with the fact. Things are happening which he said would happen; policies are being carried out at the Treasury which at least have kinship with the Book of Enoch, and, in Northern Ireland, Mr James Prior exists almost to give a *son-et-lumière* demonstration of the absurdity of the conventional wisdom about the province.

Enoch Powell, like his ally Michael Foot, uses the Commons chamber, in which both men do put a faith, to slice up the contrary view. He sits on the Ulster Bench, fourth row below the gangway, leaving the aisle seat to the amiable and not-to-be-underestimated James Molyneaux, leader of the Official Unionists. The personal appearance is wilfully un-chic—old-fashioned political uniform of black coat and sponge-bag trousers and, out of doors, a rabbinical Homburg—the typical costume of a politician in 1936. The style of speech is something for which any listener with an ear gives thanks. It is meticulously obedient to the rules of syntax and grammar; indeed he once reproved Parliamentary Counsel in a courtly way through the appropriate Minister, Dr Shirley Summerskill, for a drafting which had alluded to the wrong antecedent.

He speaks a High English which is passing, to my sorrow, out of use. He is one of the few men left who understands the noun in apposition. This is not pedantry, it is the observation of rules which, having been kept and understood, permit a liquid fluency in the English language. Humorously, there are complaints, from very good reporters who have not allowed for the complex eloquence of which their own language is capable, that Powell cannot be understood. He is conscious of the links between the quality of language and the quality of thinking. And he is once said to have remarked, 'Harold Wilson twists the English language; Willie Whitelaw can't understand it; and Mr Heath, ah, Mr Heath *hates* the English language.'

Enoch (he is one of the very few politicians whom unacquainted people call affectionately by his Christian name) is sometimes as bleak as the bald mountain, sometimes startlingly kittenish, but he has never insulted us with the meccano prose in which most politicians communicate. He is thus out of date, a Lutyens in the age of Cementation Ltd. Never mind, he is the master of the Commons. Yet how is it that Enoch, who in 1968 and for years after was talked of as one would talk of Hermann Göring, is now the popular, affable *boulevardier* of the gangways, denounced only by ritual and replied to by the front-benchers as the most serious of critics and valuable of allies? Setting aside any question of whether he was right in his remarks about different sorts of people not getting on terribly well together and having occasional recourse to each other's throats, the rising graph of his esteem long ago crossed that of Mr Heath on its way down. So, while the man who cast him ceremonially from the front bench into darkness sits in morose, carved contemplation of the world's unworthiness of Edward Heath, Mr Powell, who has a snaffled-up ferocity of his own when facing frustration, grows ever more urbane and on working terms with the rest of mankind, almost to the point of good-humoured smugness.

It may be that Mr Powell is a bit like bullion. When bad times start it is a foolish peasant in the Vendée or marketing consultant in Fulham who hasn't a little specie in the mattress or at the back of the bookcase. The distinguishing feature of the Member for Down South is not the quantity theory of money, not fear of immigration, not his observation that the cloud of the EEC had a cupro-nickel lining, not even his patriotism, now so embarrassingly popular with the brute public. The thing which matters is that Enoch Powell is an historic pessimist.

Politics is full of butterfly expectations, bright, confident mornings, plans to expand British Leyland, multi-ethnic societies and co-prosperity spheres with our Community partners. Accordingly, the man who says 'Garn', in however erudite a turn of phrase, is laying short odds with History. The House of Commons gets a full share of this bluebell optimism so that Enoch, true to his Laconian virtues, could not help contrasting, right or wrong, with the dim facility of what comes from the clip-in folders of even the sharpest Ministers. His expulsion by a Heath, between whom and himself there flowed warm currents of comprehensive mutual loathing, was uncovenanted good fortune. He became his own uncompromised force and full-time opposition to the consensus of sound men: any diligent fool can be a Secretary of State.

It does not follow from this that Mr Powell has always got it right. His departure from the Tory Party, and briefly from Parliament, was made on the basis of a wrong guess. He resigned from his Party and the Wolverhampton candidacy because, with the infallible eye of a prophet, he thought Mr Heath was going to win the first 1974 general election. It was not just a lapse of the Isaiah mechanism, it showed untypical want of faith in the democratic process. Mr Heath certainly *would* have won that poll, but only if it had been held at the start of the election. The election itself, good old Foot-and-Powell English Democracy, found him out, as the wretched man was seen trying to negotiate what he had declared to be non-negotiable, making an offer to the miners to be settled in detail after he had won the election on his opposition to them.

Mr Powell's pessimism let him down. We are stupid but not that stupid. He was wrong about something else, though almost nobody notices the fact. The riots by West Indian immigrants in Liverpool, South London (and other places) are invoked as proof of Enoch having seen it all coming. But, with respect, Mr Powell's drastic warnings back in 1968 over the immigration question were overwhelmingly to do with the arrival of Muslim and Hindu peoples from the Indian subcontinent. They had next to nothing to do with Jamaicans throwing bottles. Indeed Mr Powell once went on record to brush the West Indian affectionately aside as no source of anxiety. Mr Powell knows his India. He has a vivid comprehension of the inter-communal riots which followed the mishandling of Independence by the hero of Dieppe, Lord Mountbatten. They resulted in more than a million deaths. They make the fighting in the Lebanon look like a slow waltz, and the metaphor by which the Brixton trouble can be compared with them does not exist. It does not follow that Mr Powell is necessarily or absolutely wrong, but may suggest that his pessimism has had to be tailored to meet fears and risks, which are widely acknowledged now, but formed no part of his 'River Tiber foaming with much blood' speech. It should be remarked that Punjabi textile workers and all-night Gudjerati grocers are not burning down anything.

Another of the limitations of his record on prophecy concerns the Common Market. Most of the popular dislike for The Thing is based now upon specifically economic consequences—high food prices, thumping contributions to Overseas Aid just across the Channel in the form of the humorously named 'Budget'. Yet it was not Mr Powell who long dwelt upon such a prospect. His objection was the constitutional one of sovereignty. He had a point, of course; we could hardly be robbed without depriving ourselves of the authority to resist the take. Yet, on the hard details which hit the citizen, it was Peter Shore who made the astonishingly accurate estimates of what the cost of the button-headed negotiations of Mr Geoffrey Rippon would finally amount to.

But then men are at their best with their preoccupations and Enoch Powell's is this country. He is not a man from whom the weasel, stoat and ferret word, 'society', lightly comes. Sovereignty was a loss of England, immigration was an unEnglishing, and Mr Powell in his pessimism believes in the nation as the only mechanism which works, precisely because it is not a mechanism.

In consequence he has a laser-like contempt for all groupings and mergers. He takes a fairly marginal view of NATO, being at heart anti-American and, as they say, 'soft on communism'. In his case this means a belief that that other nation, Russia, does not impinge upon our lives or affect our identity as the United States does. Like the West Indians, the Soviets tend to be discounted, whereas the best view he takes of the US is that it is not Western Europe.

Ironically, the categorical rejector of the European idea and the advocate of an island identity is one of the few men in politics with a thorough European culture. Denis Healey has been applauded here for his Renaissance Man act, but Denis Healey would do very well to go three rounds with Powell. But while he is not, and has never been, a hater of the countries which make up Europe, his sympathy is with identity, and the EEC is a blotter-out of identity, that of others as well as of ourselves. Beyond any question, Powell would have opposed it even more fiercely if the concept had been economically equitable. He has something of a Fauconbridge view of his country, requiring that 'England to itself remain but true'. It is very *passé* of him, but an abiding cause of his national popularity. It also explains the elation which took him up near the end of the Falklands war. Being a pessimist he had not dared to believe in the possibility of our acting together for *us*, with the Foreign Office helpless to intervene on the other side. His question to Mrs Thatcher, about what sort of metal she was made of, was not resentful or jealous. After a period of irritation he had already been giving the Prime Minister notably kindly reviews (and he was of course to make a magnificent *amend honourable*—the Public Analyst's report that this was high tensile steel). He simply found the Falklands expedition so much against the prideless grain of recent years that he half expected, as did most Members, that we would be rescued by either the cavalry of ambiguity, the knights of the Foreign Office, or by the Americans. When neither of these things happened, Powell became elated and jovial, a prospect as improbable as a drunken rabbi.

There is a vein of romanticism there, so long as one remembers that it is Roundhead romanticism: puritans, from Cromwell to Montgomery, make better soldiers. The romance is of a people which 'knows what it fights for and loves what it knows', but then that description has always fitted the former Brigadier Powell, as those who have fought him have painfully found out. He is sometimes mistaken, and he can pursue a point of logic into thickets where he loses the rest of us. (He is by the way a dedicated rider to hounds.) He can rationalize, he can be narrow. But, in his luminous and sulphurous way, in a permanent condition of menacing civility, he is the leading parliamentarian of the age.

Mr Michael Foot started early and has continued late. The boy editor of the *Evening Standard* in the early 1940s has become the venerable leader of the Labour Party in the early 1980s. And the connection between the two is non-existent. Even the idea of Michael Foot as leader of his Party would have seemed a jolly little extravagance until the last twelvemonth before his election. Too large a part of the electorate still see it that way.

But Michael Foot's career is an honourable one. He did not even hunger and thirst after office, it happened to him. The Labour Party's electoral college was faced with a choice betwen Denis Winston Healey and 10 ccs of hydrocyanic acid, and was to be heard muttering 'There must be some sort of compromise'. Benn alone destroyed Benn across the last decade. The smaller the share of the Parliamentary Party in the electoral college, the larger the proportion who were set upon voting for what a logician would call 'Not Benn'. This might narrowly have been the learned ruffian, but a handful of votes from future members of the Social Democratic Party probably destroyed the margin he needed on the first ballot to come out as the winner.

Foot emerged as Residual Man—nice, affectionately regarded, with many friends, without many enemies if also without many admirers. He was also too old, very short of front-bench experience and faintly suggestive of political archaeology. Many selections of leaders are however influenced by performances in the House just before the choice is made. Mrs Thatcher had made an outstanding contribution in 1975 on the Finance Bill, all expert detail and combativeness. Michael Foot had made a gentle but hilarious speech sending up Sir Keith Joseph as the magician who smashes a watch with a hammer and then says 'Oh er I've forgotten how the second half of the trick goes.'

They are characteristic contributions. If Mrs Thatcher had Mr Foot's grasp of detail and he had her sense of humour the world would be a poorer place. Foot is a journalistic politician, not a hard thing for a journalist to say. He has always used a broad brush, regularly been very funny and frequently gone over the oratorical top. Orwell, Foot's friend and colleague on *Tribune* thirty-five years ago, once observed Shakespeare's verbal exuberance was so great that the character of Ancient Pistol seemed to have been created to catch the overflow in his bombastic and almost meaning-free speeches. When Foot is let loose on 'The red blood of socialist courage', he can be very Pistolian. He has always been an orator. Trafalgar Square attracts him as the Haymarket attracted Mr Gladstone. No talent can bear too much amplification; and too long a time has been spent on the grand simplicities which come from plinths.

Unlike a great many Party Colleagues he is *socially* a socialist and adheres to a broadly socialist mode of dress—jackets not suits, dark shirts not white ones, knitted ties and sensible shoes. The entire melancholy episode of the donkey jacket at the Cenotaph, when the Conservative press treated him with much unkindness, was a product of this pattern of informality. Mr Foot is as reverent and sorrowful towards dead soldiers as the most smartly turned-out mourner, but he was observing the sartorial practice of his own peer group.

If as leader he has not been a great success and if some of the zing and fun has gone out of his performances in the House, those who censure should be careful. It has been a horrible job. Despite the figures and the miseries of Life with Margaret, it is unprofitable to be the Opposition. Labour is a bit like the House of Usher, and it will take more than the best endeavours to keep it standing. Mr Foot does strive—and with ancillary forces like Miss Boothroyd and Mr Golding, seen on the Left as respectively the new Shirley Williams and the new Beria, he has something to show in the form of an NEC which would have graced the age of Arthur Deakin. That time of course was Mr Foot's own era of exile and rebellion. To watch the Militant Tendency being put to the sword by a man who was once expelled from the Labour Party has its own *Schadenfreude*. For Foot came to front-bench politics very late, held no junior office at all and became suddenly a cabinet Minister at 61, entering the battery after a lifetime as a free-range back-bencher. There has been nothing like it since William De Morgan turned from pottery to literature at 70.

Foot is usually blamed for the wrong things, but his recent inability to dominate in the House while coping with the leadership has something to do with the nature of his great talent. His weakness lies in the sheer facility with which he has always spoken. Some, like him, are born speakers; others, like Mrs Thatcher, achieve speaking; yet others, like Mr Heath, have speaking thrust upon them. Mr Foot would have made a wonderful Frenchman, French politics always having had a higher floridity threshold and a closer affinity to the world of letters. Most modern politicians, especially Tories, are of the school of Verlaine—'Take eloquence and ring its neck.'

They are dull muggers-up of essential facts. And it is not unkind to say that Mr Foot is a brilliant expounder of the fact-free speech. If bricks are intended to break windows (in a mild constitutional way) the straw is an expensive overhead. For the sort of garden-wall construction needed in official politics, straw of a useful, nutritious, statistical kind is essential. So much of the exchanges between Ministers and their opposite numbers consists of a solemn advance of percentiles and aggregates which meet expert rebuttal, the reminder that they are not seasonally adjusted or that taking 1971 as a base one gets a very different picture.

There are many such well-briefed, knowledgeable people about, and a very great pain they are. But given their existence, the Foot style of speech is vulnerable. It is full of stresses (in odd places) and it can be mistaken (and this truly would be a mistake) for rant. Foot is beloved of politicians and hopelessly unsuccessful with the electorate. The public sees a lifetime socialist in full court uniform. Foot's niceness does not have wide appreciation; his acts of ineptitude have been seen in a bright light. But his weaknesses are the ones people were looking for anyway—the orator's manner and the style of a Gentleman Socialist and also a want of ease or relaxation to communicate assurance.

Quite seriously, Mr Foot needed from the day he was elected the services of a Gordon Reece, the Thatcher-filter who took away her hats, vetted her clothes and hair styles and did what he could for her voice. A Labour Reece would have ordered an early haircut; would have bought mixed white and striped shirts and a few (small C) conservative plain ties. He would also have forbidden his leader, since that is what leaders are for, to go on marches or de-monstrations and would have set him to two hours' extra boring study a day until his blue-bookmanship was up to local links standard.

This was never done. Michael Foot went on his marches, remained true to himself and in the process communicated two things: that he was *ancien jeu*, a thirties radical grown old, and a degree of indignant vagueness. Foot on peace or Foot on unemployment lacks concision. There is also the question of whom the public is going to let order it around. Mrs Thatcher's manner may grate, the degree of her actual decisiveness may be misperceived and exaggerated, but she does have a touch of kingship. Foot is too much of an old-fashioned Liberal, 'a paladin of abstraction', as Disraeli called Gladstone, to touch a country worried enough actually to want leading.

Oddly enough, when he first held office, he was sometimes illiberal, heavy on the guillotine as Leader of the House and earnest to pass some trade union legislation upon which oppressive authority could be and was built. But unlike Mr Benn, Foot, however wrong in a judgement, was never a power-worshipper. He admired the trade unions because he admired the industrial worker and the unions were the most plausible representatives of the workers. This sort of romanticism is half of his trouble. He is ill suited to convincing Labour's voters, who are drifting away in any case, because he has always seen the workers without warts and from a certain distance. There are more affinities between the paternalism of the Priors and Gilmours and the adaptive enthusiasm for the working class of Foot than appearances suggest.

It is not as a stance patronizing, but it does amount to the offer of devoted patron*ship*. There is just a touch of mission politics about it; and, even with unemployment at its present level, the marginal working-class voter, with his skills and his mortgage, is not looking for Lord Shaftesbury.

Mrs Thatcher, as well as having kingship going for her, has also paradoxically more of a sense of having started as someone not too different from that skilled worker. She is the daughter of a man who began as a factory worker and went upwards. Foot is the son of the secure professional upper classes in the Trevelyan Left-Liberal mould. Good people they are, with a sense of downward obligation which in a later generation was to become an idealization of the worker.

It is all rather nice, and part of the soft top of English society, so much more agreeable than the brass fittings to be found in France. But ultimately the best-intending of patrons end by exasperating their charges. Foot gets terrible poll scores, just about the worst ever recorded for the leader of a great party, for the same reason that the broad public discounts Willie Whitelaw. Both are in the Cheeryble tradition, the good squire or model employer. Both are mild men, despite furious attempts by Foot to work up a detergent passion. Both are perceived as being soft by a public which is asking not for savage excess but for some firmness of mind. And it is not unkind to say that both are exposed by their own performances to a notion of absurdity. Force and melodrama no longer please. Other politicians like them, the lobby likes them. But to the voter they are old-fashioned sweet puddings at a time when he has acquired sharper, more astringent tastes.

Michael Foot will continue in the Labour leadership. He will get some fillip from the rigour of his startling new right-wing allies, on the NEC, and their trade union friends, who are rightly pushing him towards a more decisive use of his authority. But the sort of Left which has built up in the constituencies, and can be seen running some of the London Boroughs, has a savagery and malevolence which the voter increasingly knows about. They owe him nothing and despise him beyond the capacity of their short primitive vocabularies to express. But it is well within the range of their extensive power in the constituency parties to make all necessary tumult to do for Labour this time. Any Labour leader at this stage would have a grim time of it, and, in fairness, they might not all have been as brave as Foot has tried to be. But he must reasonably expect defeat at an election, and an early end to what was meant anyway to be an interim leadership.

His own metaphor to describe the beloved Aneurin Bevan, whose biography he wrote, was Charles James Fox. If I wanted a parallel for Michael Foot himself, I would go outside English history to, alas, one of the countries of the EEC. As a rebel by temperament, a man able to inspire others with immense affection by a fundamental unaptness for being either an executive ruler or official personage; as one drawn to books and to the simulation of action at the public meeting, he reminds me very much of Giuseppi Mazzini. Mazzini was a passionate lover of literature, indeed of words, spoken and written. He was not intended for the dull necessities and compromise of ruling. He was brave for his ends, but he is remembered as the quintessence of generous rebelliousness. That is the substance of Foot and no ignoble comparison.

A Social Democratic MP put it nicely, catching sight of a TV screen over my shoulder in the foyer of the Assembly Rooms in Derby. 'That bloody woman,' he said. 'Who?' I asked slow-wittedly. 'The Prime Minister of course. Mind you, I think she is a demonstration of something we just haven't taken seriously enough—will power, the sheer force of one person's will.'

There is a view running clean contrary which says, 'Actually, she is remarkably ineffectual. She fights only some of the battles and leaves half the issues to other people whom she can't trust. They present her with *faits accomplis* which she just submits to.'

The second, and at present unfashionable, theory notes the power ceded to an army of opponents at the formation of the cabinet. This had its roots in the absence of one man and the presence of another. The murder by the IRA of Airey Neave left Mrs Thatcher without the moral support and the clear set of ideas about people's fitness of her political guide. She was cast on the very questionable judgement of Humphrey Atkins, a Chief Whip not greatly loved and one instinctively out of sympathy with all Mrs Thatcher stands for.

The result was a cabinet of older and wiser heads, who despised her, smiled at her outlandishness and expected to be able to cope with the foolish notions of their Prime Minister. The 'ineffectuality' theory is somewhat knocked about by the presence of those wiser heads on the end of poles. The great complaint today is that she is undermining the constitution by creating a Parallel Bureau to vet and criticize the mature conclusions of senior civil servants. Though this, in its way, is an illustration of her imperfect confidence in some of her colleagues. And it is valid to suggest that some subjects have been unceremoniously dumped into a position of such radical inconsequence that the other people have been freer than they should have been to get things wrong. Her exact opposite as a functioning Prime Minister seems to have been Anthony Eden, who was notorious, in his short time, as a fusser over the small points of other Ministers' Departments.

Happily or not, she *does* delegate and has extended a wide

tolerance to opponents. The reshuffles were no butcheries, loudly as the consensual press squeaked at the time. Those who went did not go a moment too soon. Most of them had functioned not as colleagues, however critical, but as men who had learnt their notions of cabinet responsibility and common loyalty from Mr Anthony Wedgwood Benn. But then they were not merely taking a contrary view on a policy, they simply did not accept the legitimacy of Margaret Thatcher.

Iain Macleod wrote a famous article for the *Spectator* after he had resigned from government, attacking 'The Magic Circle', those senior Ministers who used to deliver to a grateful Parliamentary Party the name of the leader who had 'emerged'. Macleod, the difficult son of a Scottish doctor, and despite his colonial policy essentially a hard man and a believer in combat, was indeed excluded. But the rules which had sustained the Magic Circle were changed, and the first beneficiary was Edward Heath, like Mrs Thatcher a product of what was then seen as social outer space.

Few of the gentlemanly caste in 1975 were actually in mourning for Heath, who had simply failed. But the change followed a challenge which none of them would have dared to make, which explicitly none of them *did* make. Not merely did it come from the former Minister of Education, from a woman, from a social outsider, from a person not gracefully attentive to the adaptive liberalism then accepted as the price of Conservative survival, but also from the person they hadn't seriously considered. The emergence of Margaret Thatcher was a democratic election held by secret ballot, expressing the wishes of a majority of elected Conservative representatives, but it was felt and sensed and resented in some circles as a sort of Bolivian coup. Coming from a group of hereditarians, scared silly of the British people, this was excessive.

However it is not hard to see how they would fail to get along. The important thing about Margaret Thatcher is that she is in deadly earnest, not only , as the world well knows, a compulsive worker, but a deliberate concentrator on the single issue of the economy—until the Falklands crisis occurred. She is a bitter critic of the policies which, with remissions, have from Macmillan until now built inflation. When discussing her time in power, she talks about ten years. Be assured, she means ten years. It is the time she thinks necessary to obtain something close to zero inflation, though it is likely to rise a little in 1983.

Now such an attitude, which has begun to show rewards, is at odds with the butterfly yearnings of her old guard. With Mr Pym as Prime Minister or Mr Prior one could have opened a book on the month when he would have panicked.

Mrs Thatcher, God knows, is not all iron, but she has pinched an idea from Nye Bevan, and is determined that Conservatism, her

Conservatism, shall be about priorities, with the economy and specifically inflation at the top. To the passion for shallow options of a reflationary kind of her Conservative opponents should be added another reason for their unhappiness. Their attitudes are based upon the belief that without amelioration comes anarchy. The people underneath must be bought off, or to put it more nobly, 'reconciled'. 'One Nation' which was flashed round Blackpool in 1981 as shorthand for 'Stop the Woman', is not so much humane as defensive.

Indeed the Magic Circle is most marked for a losing-side psychology. One associates its members with a number of defeats at the hands of Arthur Scargill; of the French Ministry of Agriculture; of the TUC to whom its representative, Mr Prior, deferred on the issue of the closed shop; of the IRA, with whom it negotiated; of inflation, a long-term problem for which its short-term spirit was not equipped; and, finally and most painfully, of Mrs Margaret Thatcher who, by some alchemic means, has managed to become an object of public respect and awe, which for a 'banal little suburban woman' is not bad.

It is not novelty that does it. We have had four years of Maggie, and four years, in criminal terminology, is a stretch. It is not love. That might actually come, odd as it sounds, if the private virtues should percolate through the authoritativeness and emphasis. There are plenty of people closer up who have a feeling close to it. But time and hardship will have to pass first.

Margaret Thatcher ought on paper to fail as a leader. Much as it will annoy her, she still sounds like a posh lady. Her own Wesleyan morality about work could easily be a cause of grinding ill will, a two-way current of imperiousness and resentment. She has no great resources of humour. She is a meritocrat in a country with limited regard for those who 'get on'. She ought, again on paper, to have been far more mockable that she has been. The last batch of politicians—Home, Wilson, Heath and Callaghan—were all under fire from a generation of mockers; satire shows, impressionists and even sketch writers! Brisk, fond lackeys are not what they were, even if they are softer than the American media. Of those four, only Callaghan got out alive; and Uncle Jim would have survived on the Soviet Presidium in 1938. Politicians have a shorter life than they used to. Once at the top reputations crumble as our rulers are mocked to death. In Mrs Thatcher's case commentators *began* by mocking, but they have have not continued. Yet discounting her noisy support in mass circulation papers, no politician has been so systematically underrated by the thoughtful writers of quality comment. 'Twinsets and pearls, lower-middle-class, vulgar, hectoring, shrill, needing to be sustained by *civilized* Conservatives, reactionary, jingoistic, primitive, not very clever, embarrassing'.

Mrs Thatcher has been all those things under the wrinkled noses of the discerning for four years of opposition and four of government; and look at her. She has taken on all patronizers and seen them off. The strongest card in her hand has always been populism. She is not liked for being Dry. Though it does not offend the best minds of our generation, for whom Dryness, while it is mistaken, is intellectually respectable. To revert to the terminology of the Ptolemaic Atlas: she is popular for being 'Right-Wing'. She is a rough patriot. She would hang terrorists if she could. She loathes the Soviet Union. She has bashed trade unions. She has bashed the former President of France, the diamond-accumulating M. Giscard and made us all feel the better for it. She has a fingertip feeling for those convictions of the citizen which the best minds of our generation describe as prejudices.

Often she gives way (the ineffectuality argument) and more Indian fiancés come in, or the conspiracy of doom at GCHQ is covered up, or the pledge to meet the Clegg terms is honoured. Mrs Thatcher, interestingly, is always at her worst in the House trying to defend what the sound men, the paladins of bufferdom, regard as right and proper. Her voice glazes over; the barrister's formulae come out for recitation. She becomes in her own favourite, awful word, 'staunch', performing the role of the trusty yeoman to somebody else's judgement.

Per contra she shines like a bright light when her own convictions are involved and in particular if she has lost her temper. It is a nice, clean, healthy temper. She shouts a bit, metaphorically she throws things, but one sees no spite or vengefulness; and there is this tremendous impetus which it provides, turning her into a small tank. The quality of the arguments don't at that stage matter very much. The Opposition simply withdraws at speed to prepared positions. Fervour is a crucial quality in her. So it is with Mr Foot. Perhaps it is a characteristic of Methodism from which they both derive (and which is easily the most proportionally highly represented denomination in the House).

English Nonconformity breaks two ways. There is a striving, competing, Max Weber-underlining strand; there is also a radical element disposed to pull the mighty down from their seats. But they can blur and no one should underestimate the extent to which Protestant Nonconformists, despite the tardy entitlements of the nineteenth century, have retained, like Roman Catholics and Jews, a separate identity. One doesn't have any trouble in finding the politician closest in spirit to Mrs Thatcher. Joseph Chamberlain, outsider, provincial, nationalist, undertaker of adventures and the one Tory (if he was that) to get across to the working class, also a child of the chapel.

Mrs Thatcher, who does not affect, and has no time for, etiolated literary tastes, reads and rereads Kipling, especially the poetry. To those who have done the same thing, some sort of outlined understanding of the Prime Minister comes. Kipling was not narrowly an imperialist, he was the poet of Martha who had such biting things to say about the sons of Mary, who

> . . . seldom bother, for they have inherited that good part;
> But the Sons of Martha favour their Mother of the careful soul and
> the troubled heart. . . .

> It is their care that the wheels run truly; it is their care to embark
> and entrain,
> Tally, transport and deliver duly the sons of Mary by land and sea
> and main. . . .

He was to write:

> And after that is accomplished and the brave new world begins
> When all men are paid for existing and no man must pay for his
>   sins
> As surely as water will wet us, as surely as fire will burn,
> The Gods of the Copybook headings with fire and slaughter
>   return!

Kipling said:

> She is wedded to convictions—in default of grosser ties,
> Her contentions are her children, Heaven help him who denies . . .

and:

> The excusers of impotence fled abdicating their wardship.
> For the hate they had taught through the state brought the state
>   no defender
> And it passed from the roll of the nations in headlong surrender.

The poem from which the last quotation comes, 'The City of Brass', should be read by anyone who wants a glimpse of the Prime Minister's understanding of nations in conflict and to see why the Falklands expedition was possible for her, as it would have been unthinkable for her peers. Like Kipling, who was the product of three generations of Methodist ministers, she is the Out wedded uneasily to the In. Like him, she has risen socially and has half enjoyed, half been irked by, the trappings. Like him, she is bound up with Wesley's gospel of application to work and, we can all agree, has a preaching strain.

Like Kipling, she admires things military, respects soldiers and their ethic. For although the chapels were great progenitors of pacifism, when Nonconformity and soldiering did come together they were, like General Wingate, liable to do such formidable things as found the army of Israel. For the message of Mrs Thatcher is that if the inheriting rulers are not up to the job somebody else must do it for them. (The Protestant instinct for duty, not a mantra nor a mechanical devotion, but an unrelenting sense of obligation, is at the heart of her.) There will be fancy footwork, there will be gaps and lacunae where she feels self-doubt or where she is overreached by the Establishment with which she is on terms of cool, corresponding ill-esteem. One of her Ministers said with bitterness that she was not a Tory, 'Not one of us.' By such narrow, socially sectarian terms she is not indeed, rather she is a Liberal Imperialist, a believer in both the market and in the armed camp of those who would survive.

In the process she has made contact with a public which, if it does not care for preaching, wanted a sterner gospel, had its own notion that the Gods of the Copybook headlines had been disobeyed, and finds in her instinct to react nationally and on behalf of the people of this country something it had not hoped to hear again. She is true, or as true as she can be, to ancient and long-enduring gods—thrift, self-respect, nothing for nothing. The attempts to please over the last twenty years have made no politicians popular and made each of them vulnerable to devaluation and irrelevance. Hard times and hard words, like Mr Powell's pessimism, have communicated; and in melancholy times she has taken people (and most notably working people) with her. She has been, within the limitations of politics, honest. The waters rise and could quite easily drown her; but to paraphrase Lord Carrington's remark about the bus which is supposed to knock Prime Ministers down for the benefit of hypothesis, they wouldn't dare. We are back with my SDP friend and his acknowledgement of the power of will. After a generation of painless and beguiling options, it is not a moment too soon.

There is another line of Kipling's which runs: 'Maggie and I are out'. After traversing what I can of a broad, parliamentary territory, marked by the cartographers 'Here be monsters', *I* indeed am out; but Maggie, despite the most urgent calls from the benches opposite, is not and will not be for quite some time to come. Maggie is in!

Index

174 *Index*

Joseph, Sir Keith, Bt, 31, 52, 56, 60, 80, 120, 124, 160

Kant, Immanuel, 111
Kaufman, Gerald, 35, 36, 38, 39
Kellett-Bowman, Elaine, 123
King, Tom, 120, 125
Kinnock, Neil, 18, 32, 33, 65, 87, 96, 127, 148
Kipling, Rudyard, 168, 169
Knight, Jill, 98
Knox, David, 100
Knox, John, 127
Kosygin, Alexei N., 57
Kray, Ronald, Reginald and Charles, 128

Laker, Freddie, 23
Lamond, James, 90
Lawson, Nigel, 52, 57, 58
Lenin, V. I., 90, 95
Lever, Harold, 34
Livingstone, Ken, 64, 137
Lloyd, Peter, 119, 120
Lloyd, Selwyn (Lord Selwyn-Lloyd), 126
Lloyd George, David (Earl Lloyd-George), 32
Louis XIV, 65
Loyden, Eddie, 105
Lutyens, Sir Edwin, 157
Lyon, Alexander, 138, 139

Macfarlane, Neil, 120
Machiavelli, Niccolò, 142, 145, 149
Machin, Denry, 42
Mackintosh, John P., 107
Maclennan, Robert, 72
Macleod, Iain, 60, 165
Macmillan, Harold, 60, 79, 86, 133, 134, 165
Macmillan, Maurice, 133, 134
McNally, Tom, 35
Madel, David, 92
Marlow, Anthony, 25, 97, 105
Marquand, David, 65
Marten, Neil, 135
Martha, 128, 168

Mary, 168
Mascagni, Pietro, 33
Mason, Roy, 130, 131
Mates, Michael, 123
Maude, Sir Angus, 143
Maudling, Reginald, 101, 108
Maxwell-Hyslop, Robin, 20, 109
Mayhew, Patrick, 114
Maynard, Joan, 32, 90
Mazzini, Giuseppe, 164
Meacher, Michael, 31, 88, 91
Mellish, Robert, 19
Mellor, David, 120
Middleton, Sir Peter, 137
Mikardo, Ian, 90
Millan, Bruce, 128
Mitterrand, François, 66, 75, 79
Molyneaux, James, 156
Moncrieff, Christopher, 98, 100, 108
Montgomery, Viscount, 159
Morrison, Charles, 66
Mountbatten, Lord, 158
Mugabe, Robert, 94
Murphy, Christopher, 122
Mussolini, Benito, 50, 98

Neale, Gerrard, 122
Neave, Airey, 142, 164
Newens, Stan, 95
Newton, Antony, 122
Nijinsky, Vaclav, 17
Norton, Sir Fletcher, 15
Nott, Sir John, 55, 83, 86

Orme, Stanley, 32, 39, 43, 87
Orwell, George, 84, 139, 153, 160
Osmond, Andrew, 110
Owen, Dr David, 37, 62, 64, 67, 72–3

Paisley, Rev. Ian, 54
Pardoe, John, 137
Parkinson, Cecil, 46, 58, 120, 125, 126
Patten, Christopher, 123, 124
Patten, Dr John, 111, 112
Pattie, Geoffrey, 113